A MESSAGE FROM CHICKEN HOUSE

There are some writers who are naturally funny. Others can write thrilling plots with lots of crazy inventions and seat-of-your-pants escapes. I even know authors who can make you cry at the serious bits. Maz Evans does it all. There, I've said it – she's just the bee's knees! This brilliant start to her new series will have you whooping with delight – but even in Vi's unconventional family, life can be tricky at times . . .

BARRY CUNNINGHAM
Publisher
Chicken House

Maz Evans

VI SPY

LICENCE TO CHILL

Chicken House

2 Palmer Street, Frome, Somerset BA11 1DS

www.chickenhousebooks.com

First published in Great Britain in 2021
Chicken House
2 Palmer Street
Frome, Somerset BA11 1DS
United Kingdom
www.chickenhousebooks.com

Chicken House/Scholastic Ireland, 89E Lagan Road, Dublin Industrial Estate,
Glasnevin, Dublin D11 HP5F, Republic of Ireland

Cover and interior design by Helen Crawford-White
Cover and interior illustrations by Jez Tuya
Typeset by Dorchester Typesetting Group Ltd

This edition, December 2022

1 3 5 7 9 10 8 6 4 2

British Library Cataloguing in Publication data available.

PB ISBN 978-93-5471-444-3

eISBN 978-1-913322-92-2

Printed and bound in India by Saurabh Printers Pvt. Ltd.

For Rachel Leyshon
Thank you for accepting the
most impossible mission of all.
With grateful love.
And infinite bananas.
XXX

Also by MAZ EVANS:

Who Let the Gods Out?

Simply the Quest

Beyond the Odyssey

Against All Gods

CHAPTER 1

Spies are *rubbish* at keeping secrets. Not your big 'it's a matter of state security' secrets – obviously they have to be good with those. After all, they wouldn't be much of a spy if they posted a selfie on Twitter while parachuting into a top-secret enemy lair (#ItsUnderTheVolcano).

No – the big stuff is safe. You have to protect the code to the prime minister's chocolate safe? Go ahead and tell a spy. You need to hide the world's first laser-guided, intercontinental water pistol? A spy will know just the place. You've discovered that brain-sucking aliens are invading Surbiton? A spy will take that information to their grave. And, hopefully, to Surbiton.

But personal secrets? Forget it. If you're organizing a surprise party, say *nothing* to a spy. There will be undiscovered species in the Amazonian rainforests who'll turn up on Tuesday with sausages on sticks. You mustn't tell a spy your suspicions about the lady from the corner shop. There'll be a SWAT team trained on her pick 'n' mix before you can say 'monobrow'. And don't EVER ask a spy to keep that funny thing about your mum quiet. Imagine Mum's face when she sees her pink leopard-print knickers on the six o'clock news.

It's true. Spies are rubbish with secrets. And no one knew this better than Valentine Day.

Valentine's mum was a spy. Valentine knew this because, like all spies, her mum was rubbish at keeping it a secret. There was the time her mum got Arthur Tilsley's dad arrested at the PTA casino night because she was convinced he was concealing dynamite in a bin (it was actually his wife's disgusting sausage rolls). Or the time she trained next door's dog to sniff out explosives (and it attacked Fred the postman for delivering sparklers to No. 12's bonfire party). Or the time she abseiled from the top of the supermarket multi-storey to catch the last post (which was actually incredibly cool). Yes, Valentine was convinced her mum was a spy. And on an unremarkable Friday, in her unremarkable home, in her unremarkable town, Valentine Day was determined to prove it.

'I want a word with you,' sighed her mum as Valentine came down to their kitchen for dinner. 'This school report from Mr Sprout is terrible! What's this about you pickpocketing his board marker?'

'Mum – chill! I didn't pickpocket. I *putpocketed*.'

'You what?'

'Putpocketed. It's the opposite of pickpocketing – I put it back in his other pocket,' said Valentine, who loved to practise this particular skill. There was nothing better to do in Norton-on-Sea (or 'Nothing-to-See' as Valentine liked to call her boring home town, whose greatest claim to fame was that it was 'Home to the Norton Power Station' – and even that had been shut for thirty years). 'I just . . . relocated it. And I've got a question for you.'

'Don't change the subject,' her mum warned, lobbing the ingredients for dinner on to the chopping board with pinpoint accuracy. Mum liked to create 'fusion' cuisine that 'celebrated' their family's mixed Senegalese, English, Jamaican and African-American heritages. Tonight it was jerk monkfish with plantain fries and mushy peas. Valentine would have been perfectly happy with a pizza.

'If your first name's Susan,' said Valentine, changing the subject, 'why does your birth certificate say it's Easter?'

Her mum – Susan, or Easter – froze, plantain still in hand. That was a good change of subject.

'Where did you get my birth certificate?' Mum asked tensely, dropping the plantain before kicking it back up with her foot and catching it.

'Er . . . I just . . . found it . . . lying around . . . accidentally,' said Vi, who had 'found' the private documentation 'lying around' in a locked box in a padlocked suitcase hidden beneath the floorboards under her mum's bed. It had taken her nearly an hour to 'accidentally' pick all those locks.

'Um . . . I changed it,' Mum stuttered. 'I didn't like it.'

'I did,' said Vi's nan, who lived with Vi and her mum. 'Our family has a great history of unique names. Your great-great-grandmother was Mother Sunday. Your great-grandmother was Christmas

Day. I named your mother Easter Day and fought hard for you to be Valentine Day. Your father wanted to call you Doreen. Typical – the man was a complete idiot.'

Nan shook her head and tutted, like she always did when mentioning Vi's father, who had died when Vi was a baby. Valentine only knew three things about her father: 1) he was called Robert Ford (according to her mum's 'lying around' marriage certificate) 2) he was white (according to her light brown skin) and 3) he was 'a complete idiot' (according to her adamant nan). Valentine had always felt a bit embarrassed by her name, although it suited her a lot better than 'Doreen'. Thankfully, most people called her Vi.

'Is that how you got your name, Nan?' Vi asked.

'Independence Day,' nodded Nan. 'Indy to my friends and proud of it. Your mother should be proud of who she is too.'

'I am,' Mum replied, waggling the plantain seriously. 'I am Susan Day.'

'You are Easter Day,' Nan insisted. 'And one day, you'll remember that.'

'Valentine?' Easter said in a threatening tone

(Vi decided that 'Easter' suited her mum much better than 'Susan'). 'Mr Sprout's report also says you cheated on a spelling test. Is this true?'

'Mum – chill!' Vi insisted. 'I didn't cheat. I just "researched" the answers in the reflection in his window. I was actually being resourceful . . . And now you tell *me* something – is Mr Sprout your boyfriend?'

'Er . . . no . . . of course not . . . don't be so silly,' said Easter, blinking furiously. Vi's mum always blinked when she lied. It was a very helpful tell.

'You've been spending a lot of time together.'

'We're just . . . discussing your education . . .'

'Over dinner?'

'George – Mr Sprout – is a busy man during the school day . . .'

'I see,' said Vi. 'Is that why you have to have all those picnics at the weekend?'

'George – Mr Sprout – has a lot of after-school commitments . . .'

'Which is why you went to Paris with him last month?'

'How do you know about that?' Easter exclaimed.

Vi looked over at the kitchen calendar, which had 'PARIS WITH GEORGE/MR SPROUT' written in red capital letters in the previous month. She looked back to her oblivious mother.

'Just a hunch,' said Vi.

'Look,' said Mum, with a startled blink, 'I simply enjoy George's—'

'Mr Sprout's,' Vi corrected.

'. . . company,' Easter said. 'There's nothing more to it. We're friends. Just good friends.'

Vi watched her mum blink so hard she nearly dropped her plantain again. This needed further investigation. But for now, back to the spy thing. Time for some interrogation . . .

'Mum?' she asked as Easter started chopping the plantain, throwing it up and slicing mid-air with a small machete. 'Can I have a phone?'

'Sure,' said Easter, spearing the last of the fries with the end of her blade.

'Really?' asked Vi keenly. She was desperate to get a phone. Then maybe she'd have something in common with the kids at her school. She hadn't found anything else. Although it didn't help when your super-overprotective mum banned you from playdates and parties 'for your own good'. Vi had been at Norton-on-Sea Primary School for seven years and never had a best friend. That didn't feel very good. 'When?'

'On the Twelfth of Never,' Easter confirmed. 'You know how I feel about phones. They're too easily abused to invade people's privacy. I read this research paper just the other day about the science of hacking and . . .'

Good. Mum was distracted. The plan was working. Time to go in for the kill.

'Mum?' Valentine interrupted as Easter lobbed the fries across the kitchen into the deep fat fryer, then ducked behind the breakfast bar with her fingers in her ears. 'Are you a spy?'

'Yes,' said Easter absently, stabbing the monkfish as she realized what she'd said. 'I mean . . . no! I mean . . . I used to be! I mean . . . !'

Vi walked over and gently prised the knife out of her mother's hand.

'I think we need to have a little chat,' she said, leading Easter to the table.

'About bloomin' time,' huffed Nan from behind her crossword.

So that was how Valentine Day heard how Easter Day – and Independence Day before her –

used to be a top secret agent for SPIDER, the Security Protection Intelligence Defence Elite Regiment, but had given it all up when Vi's dad died.

'So . . . my dad was a spy too?' Vi asked.

'Uh-huh,' Mum said, turning away as Nan snorted into her crossword. 'Robert died diverting a nuclear missile into space one second before it exploded in the Earth's atmosphere. It's what he would have wanted.'

Easter shot a look at Nan, who was snorting so hard now that she sounded like a horse with hay fever.

'Why did you stop?' Vi asked.

Easter sighed and put her arms around her daughter.

'With Robert gone, you needed a stable parent. One who could keep you safe. One who could watch your every move. One who wasn't going to die in a tank of mutant piranhas. So I retired and moved us to this lovely, quiet town where no one could find us.'

'Who would *want* to find Norton-on-Sea?' Vi scoffed. But she'd been right. Her mum *was* a spy. That might explain why Vi was so good at . . .

accidentally finding things that were lying around. She wondered what skills she'd inherited from her father.

'Well, thank heavens it's finally out in the open,' said Nan. 'Now Vi can go to Rimmington Hall.'

'What's that?' Vi asked.

'Rimmington Hall Espionage Academy,' said Nan with a twinkle. 'Secondary school for spies. To get in, you need to complete a successful mission. Your mother saved seven hostages from a bank raid when she was your age, using only a catapult and a Barbie doll. All the greats go to Rimmington Hall.'

'Spy school – that sounds awesome,' Vi enthused. 'How do you get a mission?'

'You need to find one,' Nan whispered gleefully.

'No!' snapped Easter. 'Vi is going to St Michael's Comprehensive. Not . . . that place.'

'Don't be absurd,' scoffed Indy. 'Valentine comes from a long line of great spies, going right back to the days of the underground railroad in nineteenth-century America. Mother Sunday spied undercover as a nurse in World War One. My mother, Christmas Day, used her singing career to spy all over Europe in World War Two.

I was the first black woman to be recruited by SPIDER, you were the youngest. Spying is in our blood. However hard *some of us* try to deny it—'

'No!' Easter interrupted. 'I am sick of explaining this to you, Mum! That life is over!'

'None of my business,' said Nan breezily, going back to her crossword. 'I'll keep my opinions to myself.'

'I'm telling you, I'm done!' Easter insisted.

'Denial,' Nan said.

'It's NOT denial!' Easter barked.

'It is,' Nan replied, with a wicked twinkle in her eye. 'Fifteen across, "a statement that something is not true".'

Nan was the only person who dared to speak to Mum like this. Vi loved it.

'Choice,' said Nan, squinting at the crossword. 'Five down, "the right or ability to make up one's own mind".'

'I am just trying to keep you safe, sweetheart,' Easter said more gently, holding Vi's hand. 'You are my everything. One day you'll understand . . .'

'Impossible,' said Nan. 'Eleven across, "not able to occur, exist or be done".'

'. . . and going to Rimmington Hall would set you on a path that, trust me, you don't want to follow,' Easter continued.

'Destiny,' Nan announced, looking straight at Easter. 'Sixteen down, "the events that will necessarily happen to a person or events in the future".'

'It's not happening!' said Easter decisively. 'Valentine will not be a spy!'

'Idiot,' said Nan.

'Will you put that crossword down?' Easter snapped, snatching the paper from her mother's hand.

'That one wasn't in the crossword,' smiled Indy, winking at Vi.

'I'm trying to save her life,' Easter whispered.

'Then you need to let her have one,' Indy whispered back.

There was a tense silence. Vi considered doing her homework. After all, she'd need to work hard if she was going to Rimmington Hall. And she *was* going to Rimmington Hall.

'Don't you miss it?' Vi asked Easter, picking up her backpack and spilling everything out of the broken zip. 'Being a spy, I mean. It must have been so cool.'

The sound of the knife clattering to the floor made Vi jump. Her mum strode over. Easter was always working out, so she was in impressive shape. She was slim, strong, had cheekbones that could chop chicory and her short, cropped black hair seemed to get taller when she got emotional. This combination made her a) really very awesome but b) sometimes quite scary.

'Now listen to me, Valentine Day,' said Easter, her voice trembling. 'Nothing about being a spy is cool. It's a reckless profession full of missions, explosions, weapons and danger and I don't want you going anywhere near it, do you understand? Everything I'm doing, everything I've ever done is to keep you safe. You must promise me that you'll do the same. I love you so much, Vi, and I will support you in anything. But not this. No spying. Ever. You swear to me?'

'OK, OK, Mum – chill—' Valentine began.

'No!' Easter replied anxiously. 'I will never chill where you are concerned. Promise me.'

'Fine . . . I'll just get on with my homework,' said Vi, deliberately not agreeing to her mum's vow. There was no way she could.

Because now Valentine Day knew she wanted

to be a spy more than anything in the world.

'One tiny thing, Vi,' Easter said airily, shooting Nan a look. 'You have to keep this secret. No one can know I used to be a spy.'

'Of course,' said Vi solemnly. Unlike her mother, Vi was excellent at keeping secrets. The massive chocolate stain on the underside of the armchair Nan was sitting on proved it.

'Good,' said Easter. 'It's the only way to keep you safe. And, well, the whole . . . spy thing hasn't really come up yet with George.'

'So Mr Sprout *is* your boyfriend!' said Vi, leaping on Easter's mistake.

Vi watched Easter try to find a way out. She had nothing.

'Yes, he is,' Easter admitted. 'Is that . . . is that all right with you?'

Vi pulled a face. Mr Sprout was her teacher. Of course it wasn't all right. It was super-gross.

'George is kind and sweet and loving,' Easter said dreamily. 'He makes me laugh, he makes me feel young again. And when he kisses me . . .'

'OK, OK!' Vi gagged, not wanting to hear another syllable. 'Go out with him, it's fine. Just . . . please don't talk about it.'

'The same goes for my spy past,' said Easter seriously. 'George doesn't know. And I really need it to stay that way.'

'You'd better move that bazooka out of the guest bathroom, then.'

'Please, Vi,' said Easter gently. 'Please do this for me? For us? I just want us to have a normal life. A quiet life. A safe life.'

Vi softened at her mum's pleading face.

'Sure,' she said. And she meant it. She wanted her mum to be happy. And Mr Sprout was actually quite nice. For a teacher. 'But you have to promise me something too.'

'Of course,' smiled Easter.

'Promise me that you two will never get married,' Vi insisted. 'Because I'm not living with my teacher and his weird son.'

'Russell's lovely!'

'Russell Sprout? Are you kidding me?'

'Valentine – be nice.'

'Promise me, Mum?' said Vi seriously. 'I cannot be Valentine Sprout.'

The doorbell rang.

'You are silly,' giggled Easter, heading for the front door, leaving Vi unable to see if she was blinking or not. 'Valentine Sprout . . . Of course not. I will never get married again. Never ever ever ever ever ever ever ever.'

Easter opened the door, letting a blast of sappy music into the house. There was Russell Sprout, glumly controlling a robot that was playing the music and waving a bouquet of heart-shaped balloons. And next to him, down on one knee, was Mr Sprout.

'Susan!' Mr Sprout declared, holding a diamond ring. 'You've changed my life! I love you more than a blue whale loves krill – which is a huge amount, incidentally, as they need to consume up to 8,000 lbs of krill during their peak consumption period! You are my life! You are my world! Will you marry me?'

'Oh George!' squealed Easter tearfully. 'Of course I'll marry you!'

'How wonderful!' Nan cried behind them as Mr Sprout gathered Easter in his arms and Vi and Russell exchanged unimpressed looks. 'Congratulations!'

As the adults danced around and made wedding plans, Valentine Day knew her life was about to change for ever. What she couldn't possibly have known was by just how much.

Because spies might be rubbish at keeping secrets.

But they are much, much better at telling lies.

CHAPTER 2

The wedding was arranged a month later on a half-term Friday at 101, a favourite venue for spy events because of its unknown location and massive attention to security. This could have been tricky to explain to Mr Sprout – but despite moving in the day after his proposal, George still had absolutely no idea that he was about to marry one of the world's most legendary spies.

'How has he still not figured it out?' Vi whispered on the morning of the wedding as Mr Sprout was happily bundled blindfolded into the limo. Security was so tight at 101, even the bride and groom weren't allowed to know exactly where their own wedding was.

'Because there's no reason to be suspicious!' Easter whispered back, rolling beneath the car to check for explosives. 'I'm just your average, normal bride.'

Vi looked at George and Russell Sprout in the back of the car, Mr Sprout grinning and Russell looking nervous behind his blindfold. They were like miniature versions of one another – brown, side-parted hair, freckled white skin, glasses that fell down their noses and a weird attachment to anoraks. It wasn't that there was anything wrong with Mr Sprout – actually, he was Vi's favourite teacher. Mum could have gone out with Mr Snider, her PE teacher and then Vi would have put herself up for adoption. Mr Sprout was pleasant. Mr Sprout was nice. Mr Sprout was fine. Mr Sprout was . . . he was just Mr Sprout. Well, no, he wasn't just Mr Sprout. He was Mr Sprout-and-Russell. And that was the problem.

Russell had joined Norton-on-Sea Primary in Year Four when his dad started teaching there. Intrigued by the new boy, Vi went to talk to him on his first day.

'I like unicorns,' she said.

'I like robots,' Russell replied.

That was possibly the last, and certainly the longest conversation they'd ever had. Indeed, it might have been the last or longest conversation Russell had had with anyone at school. Vi couldn't ever remember a time that Russell played with anyone in the playground, or chatted with someone in class, or even sat next to anybody at lunch. Russell Sprout was an outcast. A loner. A geek. And he was about to become her stepbrother.

As soon as they arrived at 101, Easter and Vi were rushed away to the bridal suite to get ready. After three boring hours of hair and make-up, Vi had been forced into a horrendous frilly cream dress and her long, dark brown curls had been adorned with a garland of lilies that the hairdresser promised would make her green eyes 'pop'. Vi didn't want her eyes to pop. She wanted to do some surveillance. With everyone fussing around her stressed-out mum – the poor hairdresser had already been 'disarmed' when Easter mistook her hairdryer for a pistol – Vi decided to sneak out and do some reconnaissance.

Everywhere Vi went in the remote country house, staff were running around with tablecloths and plates and food – or cleaning the bulletproof doors, or polishing the two-way mirrors. The enormous multi-tiered wedding cake took pride of place on the central table, where a waiter was arranging pink and brown macaroons around the base. Vi deftly slipped one into her palm and was about to eat it when she saw the reflection of the waiter drop a macaroon, wipe it on his trousers and put it back on the cake.

'Gross,' whispered Vi, deftly dropping the macaroon into the bin.

'You should have seen what he did to the curried goat quiche,' a quiet voice piped up behind her. It was Russell. Vi hadn't noticed him. She generally tried not to.

'What are you doing here?' she huffed, annoyed that he was spying on her spying.

'Just checking the place out,' said Russell casually. 'Before my dad marries a spy.'

'What?' said Vi, trying to sound casual as the butterflies tornadoed around her stomach. 'My mum's not a spy! Why would you say something stupid like that?'

'Because she does a doughnut to park the car at the supermarket,' Russell began. 'Because I don't believe she learnt jiu-jitsu from the Women's Institute. And because when we moved in, I found a bazooka in my bathtub.'

Valentine rolled her eyes. Typical Mum.

'Does your dad know?' Vi asked. It was pointless to lie. Russell was a geek, but he was a super-brainy one.

'No,' said Russell. 'Although I don't know how. Just last week he found an old newspaper cutting of your mum in a cockpit, having single-handedly landed a passenger plane with no landing gear after a vicious gang took the pilot hostage.'

'What did Mum tell him?'

'That budget airlines weren't worth the saving.'

'Wow,' Vi whispered. 'Your dad is really . . .'

'. . . in love,' Russell replied. 'He only sees what he wants to see.'

Vi shifted awkwardly.

'Are you going to tell him?'

'No,' said Russell. 'He's happy. It's been a long time since he was happy. I'm not going to spoil it. And I like your mum. Even if she is a liar.'

'She is not a liar!' Vi lied. 'You really won't say anything?'

'No,' said Russell, shaking his head. 'I don't want him to get hurt. Not again.'

'Valentine!' Vi heard Nan exclaim behind her. 'You look absolutely beautiful!'

Vi turned to see her nan in a fabulous pink dress with matching hat and fairy lights adorning her mobility scooter. Her white hair was neatly set and her bright pink lipstick emphasized her happy smile.

'Thanks, Nan,' said Vi, trying to sound enthusiastic about her hideous dress. 'But I look like an upside-down shuttlecock.'

'Nonsense. And, Russell – don't you look handsome!' raved Indy, fussing over his ridiculous sailor suit.

'Aye aye, Captain,' said Russell, hitching up his glasses unenthusiastically.

'What's that for?' asked Nan, pointing to the remote control in Russell's hands. Vi tried not to groan.

'It's for Agadoo,' said Russell more keenly, pointing to the ancient robot across the room. 'He's going to carry the rings.'

'What a lovely touch!' enthused Nan.

Agadoo had become the third new member of their household since the proposal. It was a robot that Mr Sprout had built a million years ago in the 1980s, with a square metal body on caterpillar rollers and white headlight eyes on its oval tin head. Vi couldn't stand Agadoo – not least because it had a cassette tape (apparently this was how old people listened to music before they all got record players) stuck inside it that randomly belted out eighties pop songs. Mum had told her about some of the threats the world faced during the 1980s. Vi figured that the music must have been one of the worst.

Agadoo whirred and clanked around the house at minus five miles an hour and was constantly getting in the way. But Russell treated Agadoo like he was his best friend. In fact, Vi had come to realize that Agadoo was actually Russell's only friend.

'Hi everyone,' said Mr Sprout, appearing cheerily behind them. Even though he'd said a thousand times that she could use his real name outside school, Vi couldn't get used to calling him George, so she stuck with Mr Sprout. 'Has anyone seen my brother-in-law, Brian? He was supposed to lend me some cufflinks.'

Vi looked around at the guests filing into the ceremony room. Her mum's side of the room was quickly filling up. But Mr Sprout's side was still completely empty. Vi watched as the hotel manager – a slender young Chinese man with immaculately parted black hair, known only as H – checked the guests through the full body scanner at the door.

'They're a bit keen about security here, aren't they?' Mr Sprout whispered to Vi. 'I had to provide three kinds of ID and a fingerprint scan just to go to the gents. Did you know that koalas have fingerprints, the only animals other than gorillas and chimps to possess them? Isn't nature fascinating?'

Vi smiled and nodded. Mr Sprout was a fount of useless knowledge and seemed to know about everything – apart from the woman he was about to marry. Bless him. Her nearly-stepfather was as clueless as an unsolved crime.

A smash drew their attention as a camera flew from the window of the bridal suite.

'But it's just a long-range lens!' wailed the photographer inside.

'Ah – bridal nerves,' smiled Mr Sprout, wandering off. 'I'll go and see if I can find Brian.'

'Oh, look, there's your second cousin,' said Nan as a muscular giant of a bald, tattooed black man walked cautiously up to H and handed him his invitation.

'Mr Mason Vaughan?' H said politely.

Mason picked H up and pinned him against the wall.

'How do you know my name?' he growled from behind dark shades. 'Huh? Who do you work for? You'd better start talking or I'll make you cry for your mummy.'

'I work for this hotel, sir,' said H calmly. 'And your name is on your invitation.'

'How convenient,' snarled Mason as he returned H to the ground.

'Poor love,' sighed Nan. 'Mason was discovered washed up on a beach two years ago with no idea who he was. It's left him a little . . . paranoid.'

'What happened?' whispered Vi. 'Did his enemies kidnap him and wipe his memory?'

'Not exactly,' Nan replied. 'He fell asleep in the sea on an inflatable flamingo. He banged his head on Margate Pier as the tide washed him back in.'

Vi watched as H asked Mason a quiet question.

'I don't know,' Mason glowered, staring into the distance. 'I don't know who I am any more. The man I was has gone. Maybe someday I'll find him. Maybe someone else will find him first. But until I discover my true identity . . . there's just me.'

H paused and nodded.

'I see, sir,' he said calmly. 'But until then, I'll just ask again, would you like chicken or fish?'

'Hi!' piped up two voices simultaneously behind Valentine, nearly making her jump out of her awful dress. She rolled her eyes and turned to face another set of distant cousins.

'Hey Tilly. Hi Milly,' she said unenthusiastically, guessing what was coming. 'Great to see you.'

'And who's this?' said Tilly, pulling a magnifying glass out of her pocket and examining Russell. 'A mysterious stranger! This looks like ...'

'No . . . no, it isn't,' Valentine insisted quickly as the twins stood back to back and crossed their arms. Every detail about them was identical: braided black hair, light brown skin, matching red glasses, irritating personalities. 'This is Russell, he's my, well, he's about to become my ...'

The two girls winked at each other.

'This looks like a case for ... THE MYSTERY SISTERS!' they sang, as they always did at every family party where they were determined to solve a 'case'. Cousin Magda's graduation had been ruined when they pinned down her university lecturer to prove that he was actually a criminal mastermind whose head was covered with a latex mask. What they actually proved was that his head was covered with a nylon wig. Cousin Magda's lecturer was not alone in finding Milly and Tilly unbelievably annoying.

'We've been casing this wedding,' Tilly whispered. 'We think that the registrar is actually a criminal mastermind in a latex mask, here to take revenge on your mum. We've got our eyes on him.'

'That's a big relief,' said Vi, watching the registrar, the man who was going to marry Mum to Mr Sprout, totter towards the full body scanner. His crinkled white skin was speckled with brown spots, a suggestion of grey hair just about covering his head. He was ninety if he was a day. This guy could barely master the stairs, let alone a criminal empire.

'Terribly sorry – I seem to have misplaced my invitation,' the registrar said to H. Vi examined the registrar. He also appeared to have misplaced the left shoe that matched his right and his pullover was inside out. His biggest crime that day was getting dressed.

'I'm sorry, sir,' H said discreetly. 'I simply cannot

allow you in without an invitation.'

'He's fine,' said Mr Sprout, running to the registrar's aid. 'This is Mr Reeman. He's conducting our ceremony.'

'I'm sorry, Mr Sprout,' H said firmly. 'Your bride was very clear – no invite, no entrance. I'm merely doing what she—'

Another smash interrupted their exchange as the hairdryer followed the camera out of the bridal-suite window.

'I said I was going to "thrill" you!' the hairdresser's voice insisted through the broken glass.

Mr Sprout looked back at H.

'Do *you* want to tell her the wedding's off?' he said calmly. 'And I don't think this gentleman poses a massive threat to security.'

H looked unsurely at the ancient registrar, who gently passed wind with a smile.

'Now, where did I put my spectacles?' said the OAP, patting his jacket for the glasses that were on his face.

'OK,' said H, allowing the registrar through to set up at the front of the room, where a few guests, who Mum had told Mr Sprout were too busy or lived too far away to get to the wedding, were dialling in on massive screens. But Vi had 'researched' the real reasons they couldn't be there. There was Aunty Charity who 'lived in the Outer Hebrides' (actually undercover in Alaska) and Great Uncle Balthazar who was 'on a themed cruise' (actually orbiting the Earth on a space shuttle). Vi waved at her godmother Honey B, who was Mum's best friend and maid of honour and 'at a sales conference in Slough' (actually an active agent for SPIDER, so it was just too risky for her to be there).

'You look gorgeous, sweetie,' said Honey on the big screen, blowing Vi a kiss.

'Thanks, Aunty Honey. You too,' said Vi, blowing one back.

'Seriously?' said Mr Sprout, looking at his still-empty side of the room, apparently not noticing the large gentleman checking in a missile launcher behind him. 'Where are all my guests?'

'They'll be here, Georgie,' reassured Nan, giving him a friendly squeeze. Nan had been in charge of wedding invitations, which had been sent in code for an extra layer of security. Vi had learnt that Indy was a cryptologist – an expert in code – when she worked for SPIDER, so she was brilliant at making and breaking codes. She had sent coded wedding invitations disguised as maps, saying: MEET IN THIS SUFFOLK FIELD WITH A SUNFLOWER ON YOUR HEAD. A week later, she sent the key to breaking the code, which gave the guests the real pick-up point for the wedding.

'But the wedding's about to start and not one of my friends or family is here!' said Mr Sprout.

'I just don't understand,' sighed Nan. 'I sent the coded invites to everyone on your list.'

'And then you sent them the key to breaking the code, right, Nan?' Vi asked.

Nan suddenly went very shaky.

'Oh,' she said quietly.

'Oh . . . what?' Mr Sprout asked. 'Indy?'

'I'm so sorry, George,' Nan stammered, holding his arm.

'Nan?' Vi asked. 'You *did* send them all the key? The one to break the code? The one that would tell them where the real pick-up point was?'

Nan looked mournfully at Vi.

'I completely forgot,' she said. 'I did your mum's list, then I meant to do yours, honestly, Georgie, I really did. But *Antiques Challenge* came on the telly and you know how much I love that man with the funny hair who talks like he's just had dental surgery.'

'So,' Mr Sprout said calmly, 'all my friends and family are . . .'

'In a field,' Nan groaned. 'In Suffolk. With sunflowers on their heads. But it's not all bad.'

'How so?' asked Mr Sprout.

'The sun's out?' said Nan hopefully.

The registrar tottered over and tapped Mr Sprout on the shoulder.

'Your bride is on her way,' he smiled. 'It's time to begin. Is everyone ready?'

'I think so,' Mr Sprout gulped, suddenly looking very nervous. 'Did you know that the sensation of butterflies in your stomach is actually caused by a series of hormonal and physiological responses that help prepare you to handle a perceived or imagined threat as your body prepares to fight or flight?'

'Dad,' said Russell, taking his dad's hand with a gentle smile. 'Let's go.'

Russell switched on stupid Agadoo. Vi tried to look enthusiastic. This was it. The moment she and Mum became Sprouts. Brilliant.

'I'll see you on the other side,' said Mr Sprout kindly. He looked at Vi like he wanted to hug her. Vi didn't know what to do – they'd never done that before, so it felt like an odd time to start. After a few awkward seconds, Mr Sprout patted the shoulder of her awful dress.

'See ya,' mumbled Russell, following his dad up the aisle. Vi watched the Sprouts take their positions at the front of the half-empty room, where the registrar was patting his suit pockets.

'Anyone seen my notes?' Mr Reeman whispered loudly. 'No worries if not – I have a fantastic memory.'

Vi heard Nan gasp and turned to see Mum standing in the doorway in her long, pink satin wedding dress. She looked absolutely beautiful. And absolutely terrified.

'Oh, my sweet girl,' said Nan tearfully. 'You look gorgeous. Now let's get you down that aisle and married to that lovely man.'

'No,' said Easter firmly.

Vi and Nan looked at each other.

'No what?' asked Vi.

'No to everything,' said Easter, wiping away a tear. 'No to the flowers. No to the cake. No to the quiche . . .'

'We should all say no to the quiche,' Vi whispered.

'It's all right, love,' said Nan, taking Easter's hand. 'A few nerves are to be expected. We'll get a different quiche.'

'Yeah, Mum, just chill,' Vi said soothingly.

'No!' Easter said firmly, throwing her bouquet on the floor. 'No, I cannot chill! The wedding . . . the wedding is off!'

CHAPTER 3

Vi looked between a tearful Easter at one end of the aisle, a hopeful Sprout at the other and a furious Indy in between. This was going to get messy.

'Now, you listen to me, Easter Day!' Nan commanded.

'It's Susan!' Mum snapped back.

'It doesn't matter!' shouted Nan. 'That man is the best thing to happen to you for years! If you back out of this wedding, you'll regret it for ever!'

'I can't!' wailed Easter. 'It's . . . it's Robert . . .'

'Robert is dead,' said Nan plainly. 'And that complete idiot wasn't half the man that George is.'

Vi felt a curious twinge of loyalty to her late father. Nan must have really hated him. But why?

'You don't understand,' Easter insisted. 'I . . .

I . . . I've been living a lie.'

'So George doesn't know you were a spy, so what?' Nan whispered. 'Your father and I lived fifty happy years with him thinking I was a lollipop lady, God rest his soul! Robert is gone and the only good thing he ever did is standing here, dressed like someone dropped an ice cream—'

'Er, rude!' Vi objected, while completely agreeing.

'Sorry, love,' Nan apologized. 'But your mother made a huge mistake on her first wedding day. I'm not going to let her make one on her second. Go and marry that lovely man. Your past is in the past. Go and get your future.'

Easter looked at the floor. Something was wrong. Vi looked up at a beaming Mr Sprout and felt a surge of pity. Surely her mum wasn't going to break his heart?

'OK,' said Easter eventually, looking nervously around as she grabbed Vi's hand. 'Let's get on with it.'

'Good girl,' said Indy. 'I'll see you on the other side.'

Nan tottered down the aisle. Vi stared at Easter,

who looked as if she was about to have a tooth pulled. What was all that about? Vi knew that brides got nervous. But Mum didn't look like a nervous bride. She looked like an escaped prisoner.

'Mum – are you OK?' she asked.

'I'm fine. Let's just get this done,' Easter gabbled, suddenly charging off, dragging Vi behind as if they were being chased. Vi wasn't the only one she caught by surprise – the pianist hadn't noticed Easter's hasty arrival and only started playing the wedding march when she was halfway down the aisle – and at twice the speed to catch up.

The half of the wedding guests who weren't in a field in Suffolk didn't know whether to sit or stand as Mum raced past. The only person who seemed utterly delighted was the groom. Mr Sprout was delirious. He really loved her mum.

'Where is everybody?' Mum whispered as she reached her groom in a bridal land-speed record.

'Small administrative error,' Mr Sprout whispered back, winking at Nan and reaching gently for Easter's hand. 'But it doesn't matter. I only needed one person to come.'

Even Vi had to admit that was rather cute. It certainly seemed to work on Mum, who melted like boiled butter.

'And you look . . . outstanding,' said Mr Sprout, whose compliments tended to be on the educational side.

'So do you,' said Easter, giving nervous glances side to side. She turned to the registrar. 'Well, go on, then!'

Vi caught Russell's eye. This was bizarre.

'And who might you be?' asked the registrar kindly.

'The bride!' Easter snapped impatiently.

'How lovely, dear,' said the registrar. 'I didn't know I was engaged.'

'Not your bride,' hissed Easter, pointing at Mr Sprout. '*His!*'

'Yes, of course,' smiled the registrar, finally locating his notes in his sock. 'Now, then . . . welcome, everyone, to this happy occasion, where we celebrate the great love between George and . . . Mavis.'

'It's Easter!' Mum barked, before realizing what she'd said.

'What?' said Mr Sprout. 'But your name's Susan?'

'Er, Susan is my middle name,' spluttered Easter, blinking wildly. 'Legally, my first name is . . . Easter.'

'Wow, how did I miss that?' said Mr Sprout. Vi's heart started to beat faster. Did Mr Sprout know something was up?

'Easter?' he said with a soppy grin. 'It really suits you.'

'Told you so,' muttered Nan.

'So . . . what should I call you?' Mr Sprout whispered.

'It's Susan,' Mum smiled.

'It's Easter!' Nan insisted.

'I thought it was a wedding?' said the confused registrar. 'Make your mind up.'

Mr Sprout put a calming hand over his bride's trembling fist.

'Ah – yes,' said the registrar, shuffling his notes. 'Here we are . . . Easter . . .'

'It's SUSAN!' Easter barked.

'If you insist, dearie,' the registrar sighed. 'But your mother's quite right. Easter suits you so much better.'

'Told you so,' sighed Nan.

'Will you please get on with it?' Easter chided.

'Of course, dearie,' said the registrar, realizing his notes and his glasses were both upside down. 'Here we are. George and *Susan* found one another . . .'

'. . . at the school fete – I threw a wet sponge at him at the "Target the Teacher" stand and knocked him unconscious. It was beautiful,' garbled Easter. 'They all know the story. Let's get to the important stuff.'

'Um . . . all right,' said the registrar. 'Who has the rings?'

Vi looked over to Russell, who puffed up with his important job. He fired up his remote control and Agadoo rumbled slowly down the aisle, holding a ring on each pincer hand, while some mushy love song from an old Australian soap opera belted out of his tape deck. Vi winced. Soap operas were clearly another 1980s disaster.

'Come on, come on – hurry up,' Vi could hear her mum muttering. What was the big rush?

A mobile phone rang out and everyone tutted loudly. Mr Sprout blushed and put his hand to his pocket.

'I'm so sorry,' he whispered. 'It's my sister, I'll just . . . Hi Louisa . . . bit of a mix-up . . . yes, you can all take the sunflowers off your heads now. I'll send the cars . . .'

'Oh, for goodness' sake,' huffed Easter, throwing down her bouquet and charging back up the aisle. She grabbed the rings from Agadoo, picked up her dress and practically sprinted back again, giving a bewildered Russell a kiss on the head on the way.

'Thanks, Russell, sweetie, that was lovely – here you are,' she panted, dumping the rings in the registrar's palm before looking at the door again. 'Off you go.'

'Right, then,' the registrar said brightly. 'Do you, Easter . . .'

'It's SUSAN!' Easter screamed.

'So sorry, dearie,' laughed the registrar. 'I just can't get over how much of an Easter you are.'

'Told you so,' said Nan again.

'Shut up, Mum!' Easter whispered, looking back at the door. 'Now get on with it!'

'Oooh,' murmured the registrar, nudging Mr Sprout. 'She's a feisty one, isn't she? You'd better watch out for her.'

'She's an A-star,' smiled George. 'I'm a very lucky man.'

The congregation ahhhed as the registrar made a loud gagging noise.

'Sorry, dearie,' whispered Mr Reeman. 'Something stuck in my throat . . . Do you, *Susan* – my, my, that's just not right at all – take this man . . .'

'Yes!' cried Easter, grabbing the ring and forcing it on to Mr Sprout's finger. 'I do!'

'How lovely,' the registrar beamed. 'And do you, George Douglas Sprout, take this woman – whatever she calls herself – to be . . .'

'Of course he does,' said Easter, snatching the other ring and stuffing it on to her own left hand. 'Why else would he be here?'

She laughed a nervous laugh, looking at the door again.

'Mum? What's the rush?' Vi whispered.

'I just can't wait for the reception!' Easter squealed. 'All that lovely quiche . . .'

'Stick to the veggie option,' Russell advised.

'Mum – are you OK?' Vi whispered again.

'Of course!' squealed Easter, her eyelids blinking like Morse code. 'Best day of my life! Now, GET ON WITH IT!'

The registrar looked strangely at Mum. Mr

Sprout just grinned like the happiest man in the world.

'In which case, I now pronounce you . . .'

The registrar paused. He'd forgotten his words again. Vi watched her mum and Mr Sprout lean towards him.

'I now pronounce you . . .' he tried again.

'*Man and wife*,' Easter whispered. '*Man and wife* – that's all you have to say!'

'Are you sure, dearie?' said the registrar, peering over his glasses at her.

'YES!' cried Easter.

'In that case,' said the registrar. 'I now pronounce you . . . A. Great. Big. Liar.'

The registrar looked coolly at Easter. Vi winced as the congregation gasped. This guy had a death wish.

'I beg your pardon?' she whispered indignantly. 'Who do you think you're calling a—'

'That would be you, Susan,' said the registrar. 'This wedding cannot proceed.'

'Um – why not?' asked a confused Mr Sprout.

'Because your bride,' the registrar declared, 'is already married.'

An outcry went up around the room. Most of

the congregation reached for their weapons, but had only their tissues and an order of service to hand. Vi glanced at her mum. She looked ready to kill this guy. And Vi knew she could.

'I don't know what you think you're doing,' she said with a trembling voice, 'but it's not funny.'

'Oh, it is quite funny,' the registrar said, stifling a small laugh. His voice had dropped. It was younger. Stronger. And judging by the dawning realization on her mother's horrified face, clearly very familiar. 'But then we never did share a sense of humour, did we, Bunny?'

Vi looked over at her stupefied nan.

'No,' Indy gasped. 'You can't be . . .'

'Nan,' Vi whispered, trying to get her grandmother's attention as the blood drained from her mother's face. Easter looked apologetically at Mr Sprout, whose eyes were full of questions. 'What's going on?'

'Mr Reeman,' Easter said, putting a hand to her head. 'Mystery man . . . I had a nasty feeling you'd crawl out from under your rock today. How did you get past security?'

'Your lovely fiancé was kind enough to assist me,' said the registrar.

'Wait,' said Mr Sprout. 'You two know each other?'

Vi watched her mum and the registrar exchange a long, hard stare. How did Mum know this guy?

'George – I'm so sorry,' Mum muttered, hanging her head.

'I don't understand,' said Mr Sprout. 'There weren't any lawful objections.'

'We rather skipped over that part,' the registrar replied, as he felt around the base of his own neck. With a tug, he started to peel off his face. The congregation gasped again. It *was* a latex mask!

'WE KNEW IT!' said the Mystery Sisters, standing up to give each other a high five.

'THEY'VE FOUND ME!' screamed Mason Vaughan, bolting out of the room. 'YOU'LL NEVER TAKE ME ALIVE!'

The room was in uproar. But Vi just watched as the registrar peeled off the mask to reveal his true face. He was still old – about Mum's age – although his real white skin was much lighter and smoother without the brown spots and wrinkles. Instead of grey hair and watery eyes, this man had dark, slicked-back hair and dancing green ones.

He felt strangely familiar, yet Vi couldn't ever remember meeting him.

'Robert!' Nan gasped. 'How . . .'

Vi's heart danced a jive in her chest. She only knew of one Robert. But it couldn't be . . .

'Forgive the intrusion,' Robert said smoothly, staring at Easter. 'I do have a very lawful objection, though. I'm afraid that Easter is already married. To me.'

'George – I'm so sorry. I can explain,' Easter gabbled, trying to take Mr Sprout's hands, which were quickly withdrawn. Vi looked over at Russell, who sat down on the steps, gazing at the floor.

'Yes. I think you better had,' said Mr Sprout with a tremble in his voice. 'Is this true? Are you married to this man?'

'I was,' said Easter. 'And I suppose, technically – and only technically – I . . . a little bit . . . still . . . am.'

Vi heard Honey B's breath catch on-screen as Aunty Charity fainted in Alaska and Uncle Balthazar said a rude word in space.

'Look,' said Mr Sprout to the imposter registrar, 'I don't know who you are, but . . .'

'An excellent point,' said the man, who was now smiling at Vi. 'Allow me to introduce myself. The name's Ford. Robert Ford.'

Another gasp went up from the congregation. Vi could barely hear it over her own thundering heart. This wasn't possible. Robert Ford was her father. And Robert Ford had died ten years ago.

'You can't be,' Vi stammered, her racing heart making her words tremble. 'You're dead.'

'Apparently not,' Robert smiled. 'Am I, Easter?'

'No,' Easter said darkly. 'Unfortunately . . . Vi, I'm so sorry. I love you and I was only trying to protect . . .'

But Vi heard nothing as Robert Ford walked slowly towards his daughter. A distant memory of a feeling filled her body. Something in her knew him. They had the same eyes. They had the same nose. They had the same smile.

'Hello again Valentine,' he said, crouching down to her height. 'It's been far too long. But we'll soon sort that out. Daddy's back now. And this time, Daddy's here to stay.'

Umbra watched with an amused smirk as the wedding chaos unfolded on the satellite link. Easter Day always was a fearsome opponent. Her husband of all people should have remembered that. And if he didn't, the fact it was taking fifteen wedding guests to restrain her must be a timely reminder.

'I'll leave you two to it,' Umbra heard Robert whisper smoothly to the bemused groom. 'I'll drop by the house tomorrow for a little chat.'

Robert turned to his daughter.

'See you tomorrow, Valentine,' he said. 'I promise. And Robert Ford never breaks his promises . . .'

'You broke your promise to *me*! You swore you'd leave us alone!' Easter screamed, looking up at the camera. 'Someone turn that thing off! I mean it, turn it off before I—'

The screen froze on Easter's face, contorted with rage. Umbra smiled. That was going to be one heck of a wedding reception.

A glance at the clock confirmed that everything was on schedule. A communication from Umbra's second-in-command, Sir Charge, was due any minute.

Not four minutes later, the screen flashed an incoming message. Right on time.

Umbra switched it from surveillance mode to communication, ensuring that facial and voice distortion were switched on. Even Sir Charge didn't know Umbra's true identity. No one did. That was how Umbra was still alive. The umbra is the darkest part of the shadow. And that's where Umbra had been hiding for ten years.

Until now.

Robert Ford wasn't the only one coming back from the dead.

Umbra pressed a button and Sir Charge's familiar face appeared on the screen.

'I'm in,' Sir Charge confirmed with a smile. Umbra trusted no one. But after twenty years, Sir Charge was as close to a trusteed employee as anyone had come.

'Excellent,' said Umbra. 'I need you to gather intelligence on Easter Day – her routine, her vulnerabilities, her threat level. She has always been a thorn in my side. I have a world to claim. This time, I don't want her getting in the way. And besides, I want my revenge. I have a score to settle with her . . .'

'Me too,' said Sir Charge. 'Me too.'

'How is everything else progressing?' Umbra asked.

'Everything is on schedule,' Sir Charge replied. 'I have acquired the Norton Power Station and all your preparations are being made.'

'And the Neurotrol?' Umbra asked keenly. This was the key to everything. With the Neurotrol, the world was Umbra's for the taking. At last.

'I have made arrangements,' said Sir Charge simply. 'I will acquire it tonight.'

Umbra smiled. Sir Charge was the world's greatest thief. If he said he was going to acquire it, the Neurotrol would be acquired.

'Good. Meet me at the power station to-morrow night,' Umbra instructed. 'Bring the Neurotrol.'

'And Easter?' Sir Charge asked.

A soft laugh escaped Umbra's lips.

'Easter Day will have to wait. I have plans for her. Big plans.'

'I must go,' said Sir Charge. 'I have to see a man about a Neurotrol.'

'Excellent work, Sir Charge,' said Umbra. 'You

have done well.'

'Thank you,' smiled Sir Charge. 'And, Umbra, please. After all this time, you know you can call me Robert.'

CHAPTER 4

The day after the disaster that was her mum's wedding, Vi was back at home and doing some surveillance on the stairs, which was always a good spot for finding out what was happening below.

Her mum and dad – that felt weird after so long with one parent – were in the living room. Mr Sprout had gone out early. Having given up their flat before the wedding and with no relatives nearby, there was nowhere else for the Sprouts to go. The only thing Mr Sprout had said after the wedding was to ask Easter to return his mother's engagement ring. He had refused to come into the house and had slept in his workshop in the shed before leaving at the crack of dawn to 'clear his head'.

Robert had arrived soon after with a hamper full of sweets for Vi that Easter had immediately confiscated, before shutting herself in the living room with Robert. Vi had been doing surveillance ever since through the crack between the slightly open double doors – although at the volume they were speaking, it wasn't that hard.

'HOW DARE YOU RUIN THE HAPPIEST DAY OF MY LIFE, YOU EVIL, LYING—'

Vi felt a gentle hand on her shoulder. She turned to look at her nan.

'Why didn't you tell me?' she asked Indy. 'All this time, my dad's been alive.'

'I had no idea!' Indy exclaimed. 'Last I knew, your dad had been eliminated!'

'Eliminated?' Vi asked. 'Does that mean—'

'Terminated. Eradicated. Annihilated. See ya . . . Call it what you like,' said Nan. 'Spies prefer not to use the k-word. Your mother said she'd taken care of him. Said it was her final mission before she quit. Why wouldn't I believe her?'

Vi heard the third voice in the room.

'Who is that?' she asked.

'Fifty-Fifty, top spy divorce mediator,' said Indy. 'Your father called her.'

Agadoo suddenly belted out an old pop song about Vienna from inside the room. They really would sing about anything in the 1980s.

'What's going on in there?' Vi asked, exasperated.

'I have no idea,' said Indy, heaving herself up uncomfortably. 'But there's nothing you can do about it. What you *can* do is focus on finding your mission for Rimmington Hall. How are you getting on?'

Vi sighed. Rimmington Hall. Spy school. In all the wedding drama, she had completely forgotten about it.

'But . . . Mum says I can't go,' Vi said. 'She says I can't be a spy. What should I do?'

Indy gently held her granddaughter's chin and looked at her with smiling eyes.

'Exactly what every other woman in this family has done when she's been told she can't be something.'

'What's that?'

'Prove them wrong,' whispered Nan, giving Vi a kiss on her head. 'You worry about your life. Let your parents worry about theirs.'

Indy hobbled back to her room. Easter's voice filled the hallway.

'. . . AND THEN YOU CAN TWIST IT OFF AND SHOVE IT RIGHT UP YOUR . . .'

The doors slammed firmly shut.

'Do you need some help?' came a less welcome voice on the stairs.

'I'm trying to listen,' she snapped at Russell, straining to catch the muffled words through the closed living-room doors.

'You won't hear much now,' said Russell. 'Those doors are reinforced with an internal layer of steel – they're designed to withstand an explosion. I can help if you—'

'Shhhhhhh!' Vi hissed as she tried to decipher her dad's smooth mutterings inside.

'You can fight it all you like, Bunny. But she's my daughter too.'

'My name is SUSAN!'

Vi could suddenly hear very clearly. She turned around to give Russell a triumphant look, until she realized that the sound was coming from the screen in his hand.

'What's that?' she snapped.

'Agadoo is in there,' Russell said. 'This is the live feed from the cameras in his eyes and microphone in his tape deck.'

Vi looked at the grainy screen, which showed her parents standing at opposite ends of the room and a woman sitting on an armchair in front of them. She was a middle-aged white woman, with big, elaborately styled hair that was half-pink and half-purple, as was everything she was wearing, from her ornate pink/purple fascinator, through to her bejewelled glasses (one pink lens, one purple), her pink jacket, purple skirt and one pink and one purple shoe. This, Vi deduced, must be Fifty-Fifty.

'Well, why didn't you just say so?' grumbled Vi, snatching the screen and tuning in to the conversation.

'So, darlinks, let me just "recap" here,' said Fifty in a rich eastern European accent, using her fingers to make invisible speech marks. 'Ten years ago, you two decided to separate. Easter . . .'

'It's Susan!' Easter snapped.

'Forgive me, darlink,' Fifty apologized. 'Like the spy who took the wrong fake passport on holiday, I'm terrible with names. So, Susan, you retired and, Robert, you continued to run . . . let's call it "your own business"?'

'Let's call it "an evil empire"!' Easter exclaimed.

'You've heard of Sir Charge? The infamous villain! That's him!'

'Wow,' Russell said. 'Your dad is Sir Charge? He's one of the most wanted criminal masterminds of all time! He's being chased by Scotland Yard, the FBI, Interpol and has unpaid library fines dating back to 1987. He's a super-villain.'

'So?' Vi said defensively. Robert might be a super-villain, but he was her super-villain. 'How do you know about him?'

'My dad,' said Russell. 'We watched a documentary, *100 Greatest Criminal Masterminds*. Sir Charge was number two.'

Vi felt a pang of loyalty. She wanted her dad to be number one.

'I can't hear,' Vi snapped, tuning back into the conversation in the living room.

'And so, Susan,' Fifty continued, 'you chose to create . . . let's call it "a story" . . . that Robert had died. Why didn't you just turn him over to the authorities?'

'We had a one-year-old daughter!' Easter exclaimed. 'I had to keep Valentine safe. No one knew I married Robert – I only told my mum because we were having a baby. The best way to protect Vi was if no one knew about her connection to Sir Charge. If I'd handed Robert over to the authorities when we split up, the press would have been all over it – I would have risked everyone knowing that Vi is the daughter of the greatest super-villain of them all . . .'

'Second greatest,' said Robert. 'According to that stupid documentary, Bunny.'

'Stop calling me that!' Mum snapped. 'I'm not your "little Easter Bunny". Not any more.'

'But Valentine is still my daughter.'

'A daughter you abandoned to chase your own greed, you utter—'

'Darlink!' Fifty said firmly. 'I have successfully negotiated hundreds of spy divorces. One minute you're floating off together in a space shuttle, the next you are tearing each other apart over who keeps the satellite tracking system in the dog . . . So, if I've understood correctly – Robert, like the spy who divorced his gardener, you have decided to turn over a new leaf?'

'Absolutely,' said Robert. 'It's time I made the right choice.'

'You made your choice ten years ago, Robert,' Mum growled. 'You chose Umbra.'

'Umbra?' Vi asked. 'What's an Umbra?'

'Umbra's a who,' said Russell. 'Massive crime boss who was killed ten years ago. Number one on *100 Greatest Criminal Masterminds*. Umbra was Sir Charge's boss.'

Vi nodded knowledgeably and made a note to watch more documentaries with Mr Sprout. If Mr Sprout stayed . . .

'I asked you – I *begged* you – to leave Umbra!' Easter continued. 'You could have had a life with Valentine and me! But you were more interested in your own gain.'

'It could have been *our* gain,' smiled Robert. 'I invited you to join me.'

'I would never do that! Not for a billion pounds.'

'I'd have paid twenty billion,' grinned Robert.

'Sheeesh,' whistled Fifty-Fifty. 'Crime really does pay. Robert, darlink. I think what Easter is trying to understand is, why have you come back? Why now? Easter eliminated Umbra a decade ago.'

'Whoa!' said Russell. 'So it was your mum who took out Umbra. Wow – she's hardcore.'

'You didn't know that already?' Vi pointed out. 'You saw her chase that woman who stole her handbag up the outside of the Super Looper at Coasterworld last month . . .'

'Fair point,' said Russell as Vi tuned back in.

'Just like you, Bunny—' Robert began.

'It's Susan!'

'Just like you, *Susan*, I've been protecting *my* daughter,' Robert said seriously. 'Umbra made a lot of enemies – we both did. If they knew I had a child . . . so I stayed away. But just like you, *Susan*, I've never stopped loving her. Just like you, *Susan*, I've never stopped wanting to be a good parent. So I've had to choose my moment . . .'

'And you chose my wedding day!' Easter raged. 'You could have chosen any moment, but you had to ruin the one good thing that has happened to me since our baby girl!'

'Marrying someone when you're already married is a criminal offence, Bunny,' Robert smirked. 'And Robert Ford's daughter raised as a Sprout? You should be thanking me.'

'I should be kicking your butt,' Easter huffed.

'Robert, darlink – you say you stayed away because Vi's been in danger,' Fifty continued. 'What has changed?'

'Vi is eleven years old – I've missed over half

her childhood. I couldn't bear not seeing her any longer. So I've made a deal,' said Robert, adjusting the cuffs on his suit. 'With . . . with the police.'

'You've what?' asked Easter incredulously.

'I've agreed to turn over everything I know about every criminal operation I have dealt with – which, by the way, is most of them – in exchange for my freedom. As we speak, Scotland Yard, the FBI, Interpol and Wigan library are arresting all my criminal associates. Valentine is safe. And so am I.'

Easter let out a noise like a bull farting.

'You expect me to believe that you, Sir Charge the super-villain, have turned good?'

'Absolutely,' said Robert. 'I'm going straight. I've returned everything that I've stolen, donated my vast wealth to charity. I'm a changed man.'

'A leopard never changes its spots,' muttered Easter.

'But just look at you, my dear,' Robert replied with a grin. 'All settled here in Nothing-to-See as Suburban Susan the dull housewife. You've even got the dull husband to match.'

'You leave George out of this!' Easter snarled. 'He's twice the man you'll ever be.'

'And half the man you need,' said Robert. 'This isn't you, Easter. You're a super-agent, the best in the business. This life will never be enough for you.'

'This life is *everything* to me,' Easter whispered. 'And you are *not* going to ruin it.'

Vi watched her parents stare hatefully at one another. She'd never seen her mum so angry. Although Easter still didn't know about the chocolate stain on the armchair.

'You'd better get used to this,' Russell said behind her. 'Divorce brings out the worst in parents.'

'They'll figure it out,' snapped Vi. 'You heard them. They both love me.'

'That's what I thought,' said Russell sadly.

'Easter, darlink. When you and Robert were married,' Fifty asked, 'what sort of father was he?'

Easter paused, her jaw wobbling as if she were chewing a wasp.

'He was good,' she said. 'Great, in fact. He adored Valentine. That's why it made no sense . . .'

'And, Robert, my dear, do you have any issues with how Vi has been raised in your absence?'

'None whatsoever,' Robert replied, staring

straight into the camera. 'From what I can tell, Vi is doing everything I could want.'

Robert's direct stare made Vi uncomfortable. Did he know she was watching? How?

'So . . . you both agree that you are both good parents, no?' Fifty went on.

Easter and Robert nodded reluctantly.

'In which case, darlinks,' Fifty sighed, reclining in her chair, 'I see no reason why Mr Ford shouldn't see Valentine.'

'NO WAY!' Easter cried. 'The man is a super-villain!'

'But Robert's . . . let's call them "career choices" . . . have no bearing on his abilities as a father,' Fifty continued. 'As I said to the spy who was divorcing an escapologist: your hands are tied.'

'I want to see my daughter,' said Robert.

'Well, you can't,' said Easter stubbornly.

'Well, I won't grant you a divorce unless you let me,' said Robert, suddenly sounding very serious. 'We can either come to an amicable agreement, or I will tell your precious fiancé every little detail of your past life. Now, what do you think Georgie Porgie will have to say about that?'

'You wouldn't dare!' Easter whispered.

'Try me,' said Robert. 'I have nothing to lose. But for you, *Susan*, it's not quite that simple. Is it?'

Easter glowered at Robert. Vi winced – that was bad. But really, really clever.

'I'll go to court,' Easter sulked.

'The courts are an option,' Fifty mused. 'But trust me, darlinks, things get very messy and very expensive very quickly. Just ask the spy who divorced the fashion designer. She took the shirt from his back . . . It is much better for everyone if you can agree this between yourselves. And one important question remains – what does *Valentine* want?'

'She doesn't want to see Robert,' Easter said quickly.

'I never said that!' said Vi on the stairs.

'Divorcing parents don't care what you say,' said Russell. 'They only care about what they want to hear . . . What *do* you want?'

'I don't know,' Vi replied. 'I've never thought about it. I didn't think I had a dad.'

'My dad doesn't like me seeing my mum,' said Russell.

'Why not?'

'Because she left him,' Russell replied. 'But

because I told the court I want to, he has to let me . . .'

'I want to hear it from Valentine,' said Robert, snapping Vi's attention back to the room. 'If she doesn't want to know me, then I'll leave you both alone for good.'

'It would be helpful to know, Susan, darlink,' said Fifty. 'Otherwise you're like the spy whose wife divorced him because he piloted planes when he was asleep: you're flying blind.'

'What are you afraid of, Bunny?' Robert challenged. 'If you're so sure, what harm can it do?'

'Fine,' huffed Easter, rising up. 'Anything to shut you up.'

'Quick – she's coming,' said Vi, rushing her and Russell up the stairs as the living-room doors opened.

'Vi, honey?' Mum called up. 'Can you come here a sec?'

'Sure,' said Vi, trying to sound not at all like she'd just pelted up the stairs.

'Good luck,' whispered Russell. Vi guessed she was going to need it.

She walked into the living room where Robert and Easter sat down on opposite ends of the sofa and greeted her with big smiles.

'Darlink!' Fifty exclaimed. 'What a beauty you are! Like the spy whose husband left him for stealing furniture – take a seat.'

Both parents gestured to the space next to them. Vi looked between them. If she sat with one, it would look like she was taking sides. She made sure she sat right in the middle.

'Now, Valentine, darlink,' Fifty began. 'Like the spy whose ex changed all her clocks, this is a confusing time. But we need to understand what you would like to do.'

Vi nodded, even though she didn't have a clue.

'Mummy doesn't want to influence you,' Easter began. 'But how *do* you feel about spending time with a notorious super-villain who probably still poses a very real threat to your life?'

'Easter, darlink,' Fifty said gently. 'Like I said to the spy who didn't want her wife making artificial brains – you have to let her make up her own mind.'

Easter slumped grumpily back on the sofa.

'Your father would like to get to know you, darlink,' Fifty continued. 'How do you feel about that?'

'Valentine,' Robert interjected softly. 'I know I have let you down very badly. I should never have left you this long and I'm truly sorry. If you never want to see me again, that is absolutely your right. But if you're prepared to give me a second chance, I would like to prove to you that I can be a good father.'

Easter snorted again. Fifty raised an eyebrow at her.

'Well . . .' Vi began, conscious of every eye in the room on her. 'It's kind of hard to make a decision . . .'

'That's fine,' said Easter quickly. 'This is clearly too much, let's leave it.'

'I meant,' Vi continued, 'I need some more information.'

'You mean . . . like an interview,' Robert smiled.

'I guess,' shrugged Vi. 'It would be good to talk . . . somewhere . . . a bit more private.'

Vi couldn't look at her mum. But she had so many questions, questions she couldn't ask Easter. Why had her dad come back? Why now? And why should she trust him?

'This sounds like a good idea, darlink,' said Fifty. 'Easter?'

'It's Susan,' sulked Easter.

'Susan, what if Robert took Valentine out today, just for a few hours, so they could get to know each other?'

Vi looked at her mother pleadingly.

Easter looked at her daughter as though she'd left a chocolate stain on her heart.

'You swear she'll be safe?' Easter asked.

'On my life,' Robert vowed.

There was a long silence. Vi could practically hear her mother's brain spinning.

'OK,' sighed Easter eventually. 'You can take her out. But on my terms. You stay in a public place. You bring her back when I say. And if I get one inkling that you're dragging her in your dodgy world, then I swear . . .'

'Darlinks! Well done! Both of you,' Fifty declared, springing to her feet and air-kissing everyone. 'I must run to my next appointment. A spy is divorcing a cleaner. Things are going to get messy. Goodbye, darlinks – and good luck. Like I said to the spy divorcing the cryptologist – you'll figure it out!'

'I'm cooking dinner, so don't fill her full of rubbish,' glowered Easter as they moved into the hall where Nan was waiting. 'And she has her half-term geography homework to do, so I want her home by four. On the dot.'

'Not a second later,' said Robert, spotting Nan. 'Ah – Indy! You still don't look a day over a hundred and sixty.'

'Robert!' said Nan insincerely. 'You still do look like a complete idiot.'

'Charmed. Well – we'll be off, then,' said Robert cheerily, opening the front door to reveal Mr Sprout on the other side. There was a tense moment as the two men eyeballed one another.

'George!' said Easter joyfully, knocking Robert out of the way to hug Mr Sprout. Vi watched him stay stiff in her arms.

'What's *he* doing here?' Mr Sprout asked, not taking his eyes off Robert.

'I told you I'd come to see *my* daughter,' said Robert, smiling broadly at Mr Sprout.

'Wonderful,' said Mr Sprout. For the first time, he looked more like the deadly super-villain.

'I'll . . . er . . . just go and get my coat,' said Vi, running up the stairs.

'George – please can we talk?' she heard Mum beg. 'Please?'

'I . . . I don't know,' said Mr Sprout stiffly.

'Don't mind me,' said Robert. 'You two love-birds go ahead. Vi, I'll be in my car when you're ready.'

'OK,' said Vi, rounding the top of the stairs to find Russell looking down at the scene below.

'Quick,' she said, trying to grab Agadoo's remote from Russell as Mum and Mr Sprout headed into the kitchen. 'Move your stupid robot in there, let's see what they're talking about.'

'No,' said Russell, switching it off and heading towards his room.

'Wait . . . where are you going?' Vi asked. 'Don't you want to know what they're saying?'

Russell stopped with his hand on his door handle.

'Not really,' he said quietly.

'Why not?' Vi insisted.

'I don't need to,' said Russell sadly, before going into his bedroom. 'I've heard it all before.'

CHAPTER 5

Twenty minutes later at Café Furfante in the Norton-on-Sea park (with Easter's warning about junk food still ringing in her ears), Vi was parked in front of a Triple Chocolate Sundae Surprise with an extra helping of whipped cream and chocolate sauce.

'Mum said I wasn't allowed to eat rubbish,' she drooled.

'This isn't rubbish!' Robert gasped. 'This is finest Italian organic handmade gelato.'

'That must be OK, then,' grinned Vi, picking up a spoon.

'Besides,' said Robert, picking up a second spoon. 'You're only getting half.'

'This is cool,' said Vi, looking around the cafe. 'I've never been here before.'

'Giuseppe caters for a . . . particular clientele,' Robert said, waving to the kindly older white man with a big grey moustache, bushy eyebrows and a red striped apron behind the counter. 'This is the safest place in town. And the coffee is amazing.'

'Signor Ford!' Giuseppe trilled, delivering a coffee. 'You are my favourite customer! Nothing is too much trouble for you!'

'It's better to keep a low profile,' Robert whispered to Vi. 'You never know who's out there holding a grudge. And if I thought for one moment you weren't safe with me, I'd have to walk away.'

'Er . . . OK,' said Vi, as Giuseppe extinguished a lit stick of dynamite in a milkshake on the next table. He looked at Vi and raised a finger to his lips. Vi looked back to Robert. If she mentioned it, he might leave. And Giuseppe seemed to have everything under control.

Vi took in her dad's sleek sports car parked outside and the smart suit he was wearing.

'You have nice stuff,' she said, 'for someone who donated all their money to charity.'

'I do,' said Robert cautiously. 'They were . . .

gifts. From an elderly relative.'

'Well, can you tell that relative I want a phone, please?'

'You don't have one?' Robert asked. 'I thought everyone your age had a phone.'

'Everyone my age doesn't have my mum,' Valentine sulked. 'She's convinced that they can be used to spy on people, so I'm not allowed.'

'What rot,' yawned Robert, as a masked assassin popped up behind the counter and starting wrestling with Giuseppe. 'Forgive me. Working late last night. After you.' He nodded at the sundae.

'I really shouldn't . . .' said Vi, as Giuseppe knocked the assassin out with a bottle in a straw basket.

'But I bet you will,' whispered her dad with a wink. 'Giuseppe – another espresso when you're ready!'

'*Sì*, Signor Ford!' said Giuseppe cheerfully as he extinguished a second stick of dynamite on a nearby panettone.

'So,' said Robert, sticking his spoon in.

'So,' said Vi, doing the same. 'Why did you leave me?'

Robert gave a startled laugh.

'You get straight to the point, don't you?'

Vi shrugged.

'Is there a better way?' she asked.

'No,' smiled Robert. 'I don't believe there is.'

He sighed and put down his spoon.

'When I met your mother,' he said, 'I'd never experienced anything like it. It was the first time she tried to eliminate me.'

'That's romantic,' said Vi through a mouthful of ice cream.

'That was the way in our world,' smiled Robert. 'Boy meets girl, girl tries to terminate boy. But the way Easter kicked down the door . . . the way she knocked out three henchmen with a single punch . . . the way she took me down with a judo throw . . . truly, it was love at first fight.'

A large bomb landed at Giuseppe's feet, which he quickly defused with a scoop of pistachio ice cream.

'We knew it was wrong – she was a super-spy, I was a super-villain – but we just couldn't help ourselves,' he continued. 'We ran away to Las Vegas and married in secret at a drive-thru wedding chapel. We told no one until you were on the way, and even then only your grandmother. Indy was completely against us. She said that it would never work, that we were too different, that I was a complete idiot . . .'

'Yeah, she might have mentioned that,' Vi grinned.

'Well . . . it turned out Indy was right,' Robert sighed. 'Your mother and I are very different people and we had very different ambitions. She refused to join my world and I refused to join hers. We disagreed on everything. In fact, we only have one thing in common.'

'What's that?' asked Vi.

'We both really love you,' said Robert with a warm smile. He meant it.

'So you split up?'

'We did,' said Robert. 'I channelled all my energies into working for Umbra. And your mother . . . After an epic showdown at a power station, she shot Umbra into a pit of mutant piranhas before the power station exploded.'

'So Umbra's dead?' Vi asked.

'Yes, of . . . of course,' scoffed Robert, sipping his empty cup.

'How did you escape?'

Robert put the cup down.

'Because your mother let me,' he sighed. 'We'd loved each other once. And I was still your father. She let me go on the condition I never came near her or you again. That was nearly ten years ago. But I couldn't do it. I had to see you. It's the only promise I've ever broken. And I want to make up for lost time. Now where is that coffee?'

Vi looked over to Giuseppe, who was engaged in a duel with another assassin, fending her off with a pizza slicer.

'So what have you been doing since?' Vi asked quickly, to distract her father.

'Well, a criminal empire doesn't run itself,' sighed Robert. 'There's been plenty of day-to-day admin – managing finances, replying to emails, battling rivals . . . There's truly no rest for the wicked.'

'But now you've stopped,' Vi confirmed.

'I have,' said Robert seriously. 'Although theft runs in our blood. You come from a long line of infamous thieves, going right back to the days of the highwaymen in nineteenth-century England.'

'I do?' asked Vi as Giuseppe defused a third stick of dynamite in his bolognese.

'You most certainly do,' said Robert proudly. 'My father robbed the Bank of England. His father before him, Fort Knox. Even my Granny Doreen was the scourge of the Brighton bingo scene. You're the first member of our family born without sticky fingers.'

Vi nodded uncertainly, thinking of her putpocketing.

'Giuseppe – step on it with that coffee, will you?' Robert called out.

'*Sì*, Signor Ford!' gasped Giuseppe, who was being strangled with spaghetti by a new masked assassin. 'Be right with you!'

'If you're so proud of being a thief, why have you stopped?' Vi asked.

'Villainy just isn't what it was,' Robert sighed. 'Back in the old days you'd forge an elaborate plan, hold governments to ransom for ridiculous wealth and hide in volcanic lairs. Modern villains have no respect for the old ways. They're all in such a hurry with their guns and their bombs – no one uses elaborate countdowns these days or takes the time to explain their entire plan to their enemy. It's no fun any more. I'm old school and I'm done. That's the second reason.'

'What's the first?' Vi asked.

'You,' said Robert with a big smile. 'I should have left that life behind long ago. I should have come for you sooner. I'm sorry. And I'd like to make amends. If you'll let me.'

'What kind of amends?' said Vi. This sounded good.

'Well,' smiled Robert. 'For starters, what's this geography homework?'

Vi groaned.

'I have to write an essay about coastal erosion,' she sulked. 'It's going to take all weekend.'

'Let's see what we can do about that,' grinned Robert, typing into his phone. 'Villain.con just updated its educational resources for stay-at-home parent villains. Year Six coastal erosion essay . . . Ah – here we go. Giuseppe – may we use your printer?'

'*Sì*, Signor Ford, with my pleasure!' Giuseppe yelled amiably, smacking the latest assassin over the head with a leg of Parma ham.

Robert tapped his phone and the printer started spooling paper.

'There,' he said with a twinkle in his eye. 'Homework done.'

Vi watched as the two-page essay churned out of the printer.

'But . . . that's cheating,' she said doubtfully.

'Or "effective time-management",' Robert suggested.

Vi grinned. She was starting to like her father.

'So, I want to ask you a favour,' Robert began, taking a big spoonful of chocolate sundae. 'It's important that you understand I am fully committed to my rehabilitation. I'm going straight.'

Vi said nothing. She wanted to believe him. But . . . there was something in her gut that sensed a lie. She needed to find his tell, then she'd know for sure.

'As part of that commitment, I have been going to a support group,' Robert continued. 'It's called the Ex-Villain Improvement League – we meet regularly to keep each other on the straight and narrow.'

'Sounds like a good idea,' said Vi, putting another giant spoonful of sundae in her mouth as Giuseppe batted another stick of dynamite out the window with a soup ladle.

'The thing is,' Robert continued, dipping his spoon in the sundae, 'we're supposed to bring a sponsor – someone to make sure we're doing the right thing beyond the group. I was wondering if you'd be mine?'

Vi nearly choked on her cherry.

'Me?' she coughed. 'Why me?'

'Well, truth be told, when you're a super-villain who turns all his associates over to the police, you're a little short of friends,' said Robert with an embarrassed grin. 'I realize it's a big ask . . .'

'All right,' said Vi. She really wanted her dad to be good. If this helped, she was up for it.

'Wonderful,' said Robert, looking genuinely delighted. She put her spoon down. No more ice cream – she'd never eat her dinner. And nor would anyone who ordered pizza from Giuseppe that night as she watched him wrap the dough around another assassin's head.

'Not hungry?' Robert asked.

'It's great. It's just . . .'

'I understand,' said Robert, looking hurt. 'We wouldn't want to ruin ackee and saltfish with Georgie Porgie.'

'Don't call him that,' Vi said disapprovingly. 'And actually it's ackee and saltfish haggis – Mum is trying to "celebrate" the Sprouts' Scottish heritage in her cooking now . . . hang on – how do you know what we're having anyway?'

'Your . . . mum . . . said,' Robert stammered.

'No, she didn't,' said Vi. 'She said she was cooking. She didn't say what.'

'Just a lucky . . . kind of . . . guess,' Robert stammered again. So he did have a tell. Good.

'Robert?' Vi asked authoritatively.

Robert put down his spoon and rolled his eyes.

'Oh, all right,' he said, picking up his phone and pressing an app on the home screen. 'You must understand – just because your mother and I had an agreement, that didn't stop me wanting to see you. So, I . . . Well . . .'

He switched on the screen to reveal Vi's kitchen.

'You've been spying on us?' Vi gasped in horror. 'Using a phone! Mum was right!'

'Only in this one room, I swear,' Robert replied. 'You remember when your mother broke the smoke alarm with a ninja star?'

'Who could forget?' Vi replied.

'Well. I might have bribed the repair man to put a camera in there when he fixed it,' Robert said. 'Nice job with the armchair, by the way –

that chocolate stain was huge.'

'This is not OK!' Vi exclaimed. 'It's an invasion of privacy, it's unethical, it's—'

'Rather like eavesdropping on a private meeting using a robot?' shrugged Robert.

Vi felt her moral high ground crumble.

'I want to be a spy,' she said defensively. 'It's what we do.'

'And I want to be your dad,' said Robert. 'I wanted to see you.'

'This is so wrong,' Vi muttered, distracted by her mum and Mr Sprout in the kitchen. The sound was switched off, but she didn't need it. Easter was desperately trying to talk to Mr Sprout – reaching out for him before he shrugged her off. Russell came in and gestured to the phone.

'I know,' said Robert. 'I just . . . I just didn't want to miss out on your life altogether.'

'OK,' said Vi, watching the goings-on at home. Who was Russell calling? She didn't think he had anyone to call.

'I'll just switch it off,' said Robert, going to put the phone away.

'Wait!' said Vi, watching Russell talk animatedly into the phone.

'Would you like the sound up?' Robert whispered. Vi could hear the smile in his voice. She nodded. They would absolutely turn it off. Just after this one time. Robert turned up the volume as Russell chatted away down the phone.

'Yes, school's really great,' he enthused. 'I made the football team, my PE teacher says I'm their star player . . .'

'What?' Vi said out loud. 'Russell couldn't catch a cold, let alone a ball. Mr Snider uses him as a goalpost.'

'. . . Oh, OK, yeah, I've got to go too – I just thought I'd give you a call before I go to Tom's house,' said Russell, his head hanging slightly. 'But I'll be back in time for you to pick me up – I can't wait to come over.'

'That's rubbish,' Vi said. 'Tom is the coolest kid in school – he's popular, funny, good-looking . . .'

'Is he now?' said Robert with a raised eyebrow. 'Do I need to check this Tom out?'

'No!' said Vi suddenly. Tom didn't know she was alive. And she didn't really want him finding out from her super-villain father. 'But Tom would never invite Russell to his house. He hates him – they fight these stupid BlitzBotz robots against each other, it's pathetic.'

'Poor kid,' sighed Robert quietly. 'He makes this call every week. If he can get through . . .'

'Er . . . Mum . . . one more thing before you go,' Russell said down the phone, swallowing hard. 'My BlitzBotz final – it's next Saturday. Can you . . . can you make it?'

Vi watched Russell cross his fingers as he waited nervously for the response. A huge grin spread over his face.

'That's . . . great, that's really great,' he gabbled. 'Agadoo is going to blast all the others out of the arena. Me and Dad, we're already working on his . . . oh, OK, no, I understand, I'm busy too. OK, then – see you tonight? Brilliant. OK. Bye, Mum. I lo—'

Russell held the phone away from his ear. The call was obviously over. Vi watched as Mr Sprout came over and gave him a hug.

'George,' Easter began, 'I was hoping we could . . .'

'Shall we go and work on Agadoo's chainsaw?' Mr Sprout said to Russell. His son nodded and gently replaced the phone before leaving Easter standing alone in the kitchen.

'What's Russell's mother like?' Robert asked. 'I've not seen her.'

'Neither have I,' said Vi.

'Must be very hard for the lad. Not having his mother around.'

'Yeah,' said Vi, staring hard at her father. 'Must be tough missing a parent.'

Robert let out a slow breath.

'I deserved that,' he said quietly. 'And several more.'

They returned to the ice cream and chatted away about nothing in particular. Vi found her dad really easy to talk to as they discussed secondary school in a few months.

'So you don't want to go to this St Michael's?'

'No – it's a dump,' Valentine grumbled. 'I want to go to Rimmington Hall.'

'Good for you,' said Robert. 'Education is the key to everything. If I'd made better choices, perhaps I would have ended up differently.'

Vi considered this. She was half-spy, but she was also half-villain. She was going to have to be careful about her choices too.

Suddenly, Vi caught sight of the clock. Her heart started to race.

'It's nearly four o'clock!' she cried. 'We have to be home in seven minutes!'

'Don't worry,' said Robert, just as Giuseppe finally delivered his coffee.

'Here you go, Signor Ford!' he said breathlessly, furtively stamping out another dynamite stick on the floor. 'Your espresso!'

'About time,' muttered Robert, downing it in a single gulp as Giuseppe staggered back to his counter and sank behind it. 'Urgh – and it's cold. I tell you, Vi, the service in this place isn't what it used to be.'

Thanks to Robert's sports car – and a creative interpretation of speed limits – they pulled up outside Vi's house at 3.59 p.m.

'So, tell me,' said Robert, switching off the ignition. 'What's he like? This Sprout character?'

Vi sensed that Robert wanted her to be unkind about Mr Sprout. But instead she felt a surge of loyalty for her nearly-stepfather.

'He's really . . . nice.'

'Ooooh. *Nice*,' said Robert sarcastically. 'How

. . . *nice* for you. Do you like him?'

Vi paused. She'd never really considered it. Mr Sprout wasn't unkind – in fact, now that she thought about it, he'd really tried to get to know her. He made her lovely food, watched her favourite TV shows, constantly told her geeky little facts . . .

'Yes,' she said, slightly surprising herself. 'I do like him.'

'Well, that's good,' said Robert. Was that disappointment in his eyes? His shades were back on before Vi could really tell. 'So . . . I hope you've had a good time?'

'It's been *educational*,' Vi grinned.

'It has,' Robert grinned back. He pulled a card out of his wallet. 'Here's my number if you ever need me. I know I've not been here for you, Valentine. But I am now. And you can count on me. I promise. Robert Ford never breaks his promises.'

Vi nodded. This was weird. But good weird.

She went to open the car door, but her knee accidentally knocked the glovebox and it fell open. A small mobile phone fell out on to the floor.

'Oh . . . that's . . . just an old phone,' said Robert, snatching it and stuffing it back in the glovebox, which refused to shut properly. 'I keep meaning to get it . . . recycled.'

A sharp knock on the car window made them both jump.

'You're late!' barked Easter, tapping her watch.

'I was one minute early,' Robert corrected.

'I told you four o'clock!' Easter snapped.

'And I was here!' Robert snapped back.

'If you can't respect my boundaries, Robert . . .'

As her parents squabbled, Vi looked at the slightly open glovebox. She could see the phone poking out of the corner. If Robert was going to take it to be recycled anyway, perhaps she could just . . . recycle it herself? She could ask – but what if her dad said no because of her mum? That would just put him in an awkward position.

'Mum – chill,' Vi piped up.

'Valentine, come along,' Easter said. 'Say good-bye to your . . . to Robert.'

'Bye, Robert,' said Vi, shaking his hand. 'Thanks for an . . . educational afternoon.'

'It's my pleasure,' he replied. 'See you soon?'

'Yes, please,' said Vi, quickly putpocketing the

phone in her back pocket. She hadn't stolen it, she reasoned. No, she was being environmentally friendly, diplomatic and practical.

And, besides, surely it was what Great-Great-Great-Great-Great-Great-Great-Great-Great-Grandad Highwayman would have wanted.

CHAPTER 6

'So . . . ?' asked Easter over dinner with the Sprouts, trying and failing to sound casual. 'What did you do?'

Vi guessed it wasn't a good time to admit she'd spent all afternoon in an assassin-filled ice-cream parlour.

'You don't seem very hungry,' Easter prompted. 'I hope Robert didn't upset you?'

'No,' said Vi quickly, her stomach groaning as she forced saltfish haggis down on top of the chocolate sundae.

'You had a good time, then?' Easter asked.

'Yeah, it was fine,' Vi replied.

'Fine?' chirped Easter. 'Fine as in good, or fine as in . . .'

'Just fine!'

'Easter,' said Nan, giving her the 'enough already' look.

'Great,' said Easter, giving Nan the '*I'll* decide when it's enough' look. 'I'm so pleased. And my name is Susan!'

Mr Sprout's phone beeped.

'No phones at the table!' Easter snapped without thinking.

'Fine,' said Mr Sprout, standing up. 'I'll take this outside.'

'No, George! I didn't mean . . .' Easter pleaded, trying to hold his hand.

'I wasn't hungry anyway,' said Mr Sprout coldly, snatching it away.

He walked out of the kitchen, followed by Easter's sad eyes. Vi hated the awkward vibe. But at least it might distract her mother from her interrogation.

Or not.

'Well,' Easter started again, 'what did you talk about?'

'Stuff,' shrugged Vi.

'Did you talk about me?' Easter asked innocently.

'Not really,' said Vi, hoping her new phone was switched off. She had no plans to tell her mum about that either.

'You know,' Easter began, 'if you don't want to see Robert again, you don't have to. If it's too upsetting, or you don't like him, or he smells weird, or . . .'

'Easter!' Nan said more forcibly, giving her daughter the 'this is definitely enough' look.

Easter let out something between a snort and a sigh.

'It's Susan,' she grumbled, but said nothing more. Vi was very happy to let the conversation die as Mr Sprout came back into the kitchen.

'Are you ready to go to Mum's?' Mr Sprout asked Russell, whose suitcase had been by the front door since Vi got home.

Russell nodded keenly.

'Yup,' he grinned, gobbling down his haggis. 'I get to sleep on Lucas's floor – Mum's using the spare room for storage, but that's OK as it'll be like camping – then tomorrow, we're going to SplashZone to do waterslides, then we're going bowling, then we're going for burgers at Burger World. It's going to be so epic!'

Vi had never seen Russell so animated. Although she'd also never seen him spend the weekend with his mum.

'Great,' said Mr Sprout, looking anything but. Vi didn't know the specifics of Mr Sprout's divorce from Russell's mum, but she sensed it was a bad one. Lots of her classmates had divorced parents and there was a whole scale of being a divorced kid. There was Austin, whose parents were still such good friends they went on holiday with Austin and his sister, even though they were both married to other people. Then there was Zara, whose parents had to come to the school play on different nights after a massive fight in the middle of *Peter Pan*. As Vi watched her mum poke a piece of saltfish around her plate, she wondered where on the Austin/Zara scale her parents would end up.

The doorbell rang and Russell shot out of his seat.

'I'll go,' he said, already gone.

Vi was curious. What was Russell's mum like? She couldn't imagine Russell having a mum. He seemed more like he'd been spawned in a laboratory.

Easter got up and tried to put her arms around Mr Sprout. He swerved her at the last minute. Vi had found it pretty gross when her mum and Mr Sprout were all over each other. But it was better than this.

'It's for you,' said Russell flatly, coming into the kitchen followed by Honey B, Easter's best friend and Vi's godmother. Honey looked her usual scruffy self, strands of her blonde hair dropping on to white cheeks that had a messy splash of pink blusher across them, her glasses refusing to sit on her nose and her black suit refusing to fit any part of her body. The familiar scent of roses followed her – Honey always smelt like roses. She winked at Vi and secretly handed her a bag of sweets behind her back. Aunty Honey was the best.

'Hey you,' said Easter, giving her bestie a hug. 'You must have read my mind – I was going to call you tomorrow, I really need a rant. Coffee?'

'Thanks,' said Honey darkly. 'But this isn't a social call, Easter . . . erm, Susan. This is business.'

Vi watched her mum's face tilt in curiosity. Honey B was still an active agent for SPIDER. This was spy business. But what did she want with Mum?

'Er . . . don't mind me, I was just heading out to the shed,' said Mr Sprout awkwardly.

'You girls have fun catching up,' said Nan, gesturing towards Agadoo and winking at Vi.

'Er . . . I'm going to my room,' said Vi, knowing that Agadoo's screen was sitting outside Russell's bedroom. 'Geography homework.'

She pelted upstairs, grabbed the monitor and shut herself in her bedroom, hastily stuffing the earphones into her ears.

'Are we secure?' Honey asked once the back door had closed behind Mr Sprout.

Easter nodded. Honey went to the cupboard under the sink – where apparently a fully grown man had been hiding the entire time. In fact, he wasn't that fully grown, he was rather short with too much hair for his small head. His brown hair sprouted out of his lined white face like brown leaves on an out-of-date parsnip, a bushy moustache adding an unnecessary extra layer of hair over his lip. He was edgy and nervous, his head twitching as he took in every detail of their unremarkable kitchen in his better-fitting black suit.

'We have a door,' said Easter flatly as Honey opened the ironing board cupboard, to reveal a second man. He was similar in stature to the first, dressed entirely in black, including his long leather coat and an eye patch over his left eye, leaving his right to slowly survey everything in the room as he limped out of the cupboard. The small amount of visible brown skin on his face and hands was scarred and marked and Vi wasn't sure, but it looked as though his right hand only had four fingers.

'What are you doing here?' Easter sighed.

'SPIDER protocol dictates that agents should conceal themselves wherever possible,' said the parsnip.

'Easter – this is my new boss, Walter Toppington,' Honey introduced.

'Code names only, Agent Unicorn!' the parsnip chided, pulling some papers out of his briefcase.

'Sorry,' bumbled Honey nervously. 'Lynx, this is The Cardinal . . .'

'It's Susan,' Mum corrected firmly as she shook the parsnip's hand. 'Lynx retired ten years ago.'

Vi nodded admiringly. Agent Lynx. That was a cool spy name.

'Protocol dictates that only code names are to be used between SPIDER operatives,' The Cardinal snapped. 'I'd expect an agent of your calibre to remember that, Lynx.'

'And this,' said Honey, pushing her glasses up her nose nervously as she gestured to the other man, 'is Isaac Payne – I mean, this is The Wolf.'

Easter went to shake hands, but The Wolf simply nodded at her. Vi looked at the three SPIDER agents standing in a row in the kitchen. They were all of similar height and build – SPIDER clearly had a type.

'What do you think you're doing?' came her nan's voice, making Vi jump. She tried to switch the screen off.

'Um . . . er . . . nothing . . . just watching . . . some . . . TV.'

Nan raised an eyebrow.

'Never kid a kidder, kid,' she said, sitting down on the bed. 'I meant, why didn't you wait for me? Give me one of those.'

Nan settled an earphone in her ear and looked intently at the screen.

'So, what can I do for you?' Easter asked cautiously.

The Cardinal nodded at Honey B.

'OK,' said Honey, taking a deep breath. 'Easter . . . Susan . . . I don't know how to tell you this, but we've received intelligence at SPIDER that someone from your past has resurfaced. I wanted you to be the first to know.'

'Well, you're a bit late,' said Easter, taking a sip of her coffee. 'You saw the wedding – I'm painfully aware that Robert is back and thinks he can just swan in and turn Vi's life upside—'

'Not Robert,' said Honey grimly. 'Umbra.'

The screen was a little grainy and the picture was unfocused. But Vi could still see the blood drain from her mother's face.

'No,' she whispered. 'That's not possible. I—'

'Shot Umbra into piranha-infested waters at an exploding power station ten years ago,' Honey interrupted. 'I know. But somehow it looks like Umbra survived. And is back in business.'

'How?' said Easter, aghast. 'How do you know this?'

The Cardinal opened his laptop. Vi zoomed in to see what was on the screen. It was a film of a laboratory rat at the start of an obstacle course.

'For some time now, we've been aware of a new kind of threat,' The Cardinal began. 'It's called "Neuroterror". It's . . .'

'. . . the power to control someone's mind to make them do whatever they are told,' Easter said as the rat started running around the obstacle course.

Honey and The Cardinal looked at her.

'What?' Easter shrugged. 'I still read *Spy Digest*.'

'Well, I doubt you'll be aware that, six months ago, one device successfully achieved the ability to control the human mind,' The Cardinal said with a superior tone. 'It's called . . .'

'The Neurotrol,' Easter nodded. 'A powerful microchip capable of manipulating adult brainwaves, with the subject unaware they are being controlled. Only one known to exist, but potentially catastrophic as it is small enough to be concealed in any device that transmits radio waves – a remote control, a phone, a microwave . . . In the wrong hands, someone could replicate the tech and control the minds of everyone on the planet.'

The agents looked at her again.

'I like to keep on top of current research,' shrugged Easter. 'What about it?'

'The Neurotrol works by using radio waves to interfere with brainwaves, making its subjects super-susceptible to suggestion, like hypnosis,' The Cardinal continued suspiciously. 'Any adult in range – mercifully, the tech appears harmless to children – will do anything they are instructed to do.'

Vi watched as the scientists fired commands at the rat, making it cartwheel, backflip and ballroom dance. This was no ordinary rat – this was Super Rat.

'Scary stuff,' said Easter. 'This technology could enslave the minds of millions.'

'It gets worse,' said Honey B, gesturing to the screen. Vi squinted in.

Super Rat was shaking uncontrollably. His whole body started to pulsate and quiver, as though he was filled with volcanic lava. He squealed horribly.

'Quite by accident,' The Cardinal continued, 'the scientists discovered that if exposed to the Neurotrol for more than a few minutes, the brain just can't handle it. And so it simply . . .'

There was a horrible popping sound on the screen. Vi turned away. When she looked back, there was no more Super Rat. More Super . . . Splat.

'. . . explodes,' said Honey, wrinkling her nose. Easter replaced the haggis she had been nibbling on with a small retch.

'Lovely,' said Easter, wiping her hands. 'But what has this got to do with Umbra?'

'The Neurotrol has been stolen,' Honey B explained. 'We need to find it. Fast.'

'Umbra took it?' Easter asked.

'We have a strong suspicion,' said The Cardinal, handing Easter a file. 'We got these pictures from security cameras near the lab on the night of the robbery. Recognize him?'

Easter squinted at the picture and so did Vi.

'Frankie the Fence,' sighed Easter.

'Who's that?' Vi asked her nan.

'Infamous burglar-for-hire,' Indy explained. 'Known associate of Umbra. The man's a walking crime scene.'

'Have you taken him in for questioning?' Easter asked Honey.

'Of course we have,' said The Cardinal. 'Questioned him myself. He said he was in the area at a pub quiz.'

'And you believed him?' Easter asked.

'His alibi checked out,' said Honey B. 'But a few days ago, we were alerted to some sizeable activity on an old bank account we've been monitoring. The transaction was for this building.'

Easter looked at the picture and so did Vi.

'Norton Power Station,' said Easter uncertainly. 'It could be coincidence. Property developers will buy anything these days.'

'It could be,' Honey B continued. 'But the company that bought it – Rumba Ltd? It's an anagram of Umbra.'

'So . . .' said Easter.

'And the company logo?' Honey held up a piece of paper. It was two circles joined by intersecting lines. Easter looked at it aghast.

'What's that?' Vi asked Nan.

'It represents the darkest part of a shadow,' sighed Indy. 'It's the mark of Umbra.'

'We believe Umbra is planning a comeback,' said Honey. 'And if so, I can guarantee that revenge on Easter Day will be a top priority.'

'It's Agent Lynx!' snapped The Cardinal.

'It's Susan,' said Mum distractedly. 'Are you sure? Are you sure Umbra's back? Does Robert know? Is he still . . . I have to protect Vi . . .'

'We're not certain of anything,' said The Cardinal. 'But something doesn't add up. The power station, the bank account, the missing Neurotrol, Frankie . . . When you eliminated Umbra, no body was ever found. We can't rule Umbra out at this stage.'

'Wow,' said Easter, sitting back in her chair. 'Umbra. This is huge.'

'Indeed,' The Cardinal replied. 'Which is why, Agent Lynx, we need you back.'

Easter stopped and stared at the agents.

'What?' she said. 'I've been retired for ten years, I can't—'

'Easter . . . Susan . . . you are the best of the best,' said Honey, leaning forward and taking her best friend's hand. 'I learnt everything from you. You know Umbra better than anyone. You're the only one who can help us.'

'No,' said Easter firmly.

'Agent Lynx!' snapped The Cardinal. 'The safety of the world is at stake here, don't you—'

'NO!' shouted Easter. 'I'm sorry for your troubles, but SPIDER has other agents. I only have one daughter. And the safety of her world is my only concern. I left espionage to protect her. And I'm not going back, not—'

The phone rang, cutting Easter off mid-rant. For a moment no one moved.

'I need to get that,' Easter sighed, 'it's probably

. . . Hello? Oh, Genevieve . . . I'll just get him.'

She held the phone to her chest.

'Russell!' Easter called out. 'Russell! Phone for you! It's your mum.'

Russell came bounding in, looking slightly confused by all the people in the kitchen, before Easter handed him the receiver with a smile, giving Honey a grim look as Russell passed.

'Hi Mum,' beamed Russell. 'Don't worry if you're running late, I know the traffic's really bad, we always get stuck in—'

Vi watched as Russell's face slowly crumpled, like it was melting from the inside. His whole body sagged, as though someone had turned his bones to jelly.

'Oh,' he said eventually.

'That poor child,' said Nan, shaking her head as Easter left the kitchen.

'What? What's happened?' asked Vi, trying to make out Russell's tiny voice.

'No, it's OK,' said Russell so quietly Vi could barely hear him. 'I understand. It's not your fault Lucas has a cold. Perhaps we can do it another . . . oh, OK, tell him I said hi. And I hope he gets better . . .'

Russell pulled the phone away from his ear. The call was over.

Vi looked at Russell's expressionless face. But it didn't need any expression for her to understand how he must be feeling.

'Hey fella,' said Mr Sprout, walking into the kitchen with Easter and placing the phone gently back on the wall. 'I could really use your help with Agadoo's weapon pack for BlitzBotz. I can't get the fire jets to go straight – the shed wall's covered in scorch marks . . .'

'I need to go and unpack,' sniffed Russell, trudging out of the kitchen. 'I'll be there in a minute.'

Vi heard him come upstairs with his suitcase. She opened her bedroom door.

'I'm really sorry, Russell,' she whispered as he passed her room.

The only answer was the click of a bedroom door. She considered going after him. But there was only one person Russell wanted right now. And it wasn't Vi.

She heard Easter showing the SPIDER agents out.

'I'm sorry,' she heard her mum say. 'And good luck.'

The Cardinal stormed out of the house, The Wolf limped more slowly behind. Honey held back and Easter gave her a hug.

'We don't need luck,' sighed Honey. 'We need you.'

'I can't,' said Easter. 'I'm sorry, Honey.'

Vi watched as Honey nodded and followed her colleagues out of the door.

'Well, there you have it,' said Nan, easing herself off the bed.

'Have what?' asked Vi.

'Your mission!' Nan cried. 'You need to find that Neurotrol. That's your ticket to Rimmington Hall. Come with me to Autumn Leaves tomorrow. I have something that might help you.'

Vi smiled to herself. Nan was right. This was it. This was how she became a spy.

The Neurotrol mission might not be for Easter.

But Valentine Day was more than happy to accept it.

Umbra looked around the abandoned Norton Power Station with a satisfied smile. This was the perfect place to exact revenge on Easter Day. The scene was nearly set. Umbra had been waiting ten years for the perfect moment. And the perfect moment was coming. The second Robert handed over the Neurotrol tonight, everything would be in place . . .

The phone rang unexpectedly. Umbra didn't like unexpected.

'Robert? Where are you? I'm waiting.'

There was silence at the other end. Umbra didn't like silences either.

'I'm not coming,' Robert replied. 'There's been a . . . complication.'

Umbra scowled. Complications were the worst of all.

'Define "complication".'

'The Neurotrol – I don't have it,' Robert confessed.

'You didn't acquire it?' Umbra snapped. 'This is the first time you have disappointed me, Robert. There had better not be a second.'

'I did acquire it,' said Robert plainly. 'But it's been . . . stolen. Temporarily. I'll get it back. Tomorrow.'

'Who would dare to steal from me?' roared Umbra. 'I thought you had taken care of all our enemies. I'm warning you, Robert, I have no tolerance for incompetence.'

'This isn't an enemy,' Robert replied hesitantly. 'And I'll deal with her . . .'

'How could you be so careless? I warned you that parenthood would make you sloppy.'

Umbra stopped. *Her*. Suddenly all was clear. So that's why Robert was being unusually cagey.

'The girl. Your daughter. She has my Neurotrol . . .'

'I'll get it back,' said Robert quickly. 'She's just a child – she has no idea what it is. Don't worry – it'll be like taking candy from a baby. You'll have your Neurotrol tomorrow.'

'I better had. There is no place for sentimentality in my organization,' said Umbra. 'Let me be very clear: if you don't get the Neurotrol, Robert, I will. And I can promise you that if I have to get involved, candy will be the least of Valentine Day's problems.'

CHAPTER 7

After a miserable Sunday at home, with Easter moping in the kitchen, Russell moping in his bedroom and Mr Sprout moping in the shed, Vi was almost relieved to be going back to school on Monday morning.

'Have you got your geography assignments?' Easter asked in the car. Mr Sprout had cycled to school before they'd even got up, Vi suspected, to avoid Easter.

'Yes,' said Russell.

'Sure,' said Vi quickly. It wasn't a lie – so she hadn't *done* the assignment. But she did *have* it. Thanks, Robert.

'Good,' said Easter, pulling up outside the school. 'Education is the key to everything.'

'You sound just like my dad,' Vi said

thoughtlessly, immediately wishing she could suck the words back.

'I do not!' Easter huffed. 'I'm nothing like your father. He's . . .'

'Mum – chill,' said Vi quickly, jumping out of the car. 'Gotta go.'

'I'll pick you up after school!' Easter shouted after her as Vi walked into the playground with Russell. 'I love you! Stay safe!'

Vi looked around at the kids congregating in their groups. There was the book club, the sporty kids, the arts and crafts gang . . . Vi had tried all of them during her years at school, and she had never quite fitted in with any of them. Easter's ban on playdates and sleepovers hadn't helped – but Vi had never really found her crowd. Now she knew more about herself, perhaps she was just too much of a muddle to fit anywhere. Being part-spy, part-villain was certainly making life less boring. But it wasn't making it any less lonely.

Maybe having a phone would help. She hadn't dared get it out at home – her mum had a sixth sense when Vi was doing something she shouldn't, so she'd not had a chance to play with it. She pulled it out of her backpack.

'Where did you get that?' Russell asked. 'I thought your mum—'

'Robert,' said Vi, trying to figure out how to switch on the phone. Perhaps it was that button there?

'Oh Em Gee,' droned a voice behind her and Russell before Vi could press it. 'It's the Saddems Family. Eurgh – where did you get that phone? 1992? It's soooo out.'

Vi stuffed the phone back in her bag and turned around to face Sally, the most popular girl in school. She was pretty (on the outside, at least – her flawless blonde hair around her flawless white face did a great job of concealing her deeply flawed personality behind her hard blue eyes), she was rich and she was mean. Sally constantly proclaimed what was 'in' and what was 'out' – and it could change at any time. She ruled the playground and whoever she decided to be friends with suddenly became the second most popular girl in school. It was unfair and it was undeserved. And secretly Vi was desperate for it.

'How was the wedding?' asked a second voice, the one that always made Vi feel a bit funny in her tummy. It was Tom, the most popular boy in school – and Sally's twin brother. 'So you're a Sprout now? Hey, Valentine Sprout.'

'Actually, no,' said Vi, trying not to stare at Tom's lovely blue eyes.

'The wedding was . . . cancelled,' said Russell awkwardly.

'OH EM GEE!' Sally repeated. 'The freak speaks.'

'Rotten Sprout lets it out,' said Tom, running a hand through his own flawless blond hair. Like Russell, Tom was mad into BlitzBotz – the two regularly came up against one another in battles. But Tom's money meant that he could afford the tech to beat Russell in the championship for the past two years. And he wasn't going to let Russell forget it.

'Say, as you've had such a rough weekend, perhaps we should invite you two to our BlitzBotz party to make you feel better?'

Sally held out a golden envelope and Vi felt her breath stick in her throat. Tom and Sally's parties were the stuff of legend – only the 'in' kids were invited and they were the talk of the playground for weeks. Easter always said there were much more important things than being invited to a party. But at that moment Vi couldn't think of a single one.

She reached her hand towards the envelope.

'Actually,' said Sally, snatching it away just as Vi's fingers made contact, 'maybe not. Oh dear. That's your second cancelled party this week. Poor rotten Sprouts.'

'Let's go,' said Russell, pushing past Sally and Tom towards class.

'You in a hurry, Sprouty?' Tom taunted. 'Cos you're not going to get very far without your books.'

With a nasty tug, Tom snatched open the back of Russell's backpack, letting his books spill all over the playground. Russell stopped. Had this been unusual, it might have been upsetting. But for Russell, it was neither. Vi helped him pick up his books.

'Thanks,' said Russell, stuffing his bag with a resigned sigh as Tom and Sally ran laughing into class.

'Hey – be grateful you got into the Tech Academy,' said Vi. Russell's mega-brain had secured him a scholarship to a prestigious science and technology academy. At least he'd be away from

Tom and Sally. Which was more than Vi had to look forward to if she didn't get into Rimmington Hall. She needed to do some work on the Neurotrol mission. But how?

'I am,' said Russell, hitching his glasses up his nose. 'Believe me.'

They headed towards their classroom.

'So how was it?' Russell began. 'With your dad?'

'He seems . . . OK,' said Vi honestly. 'What's your mum like?'

'She's awesome,' said Russell with a small smile. 'She's funny and silly and cool and . . .'

'Good morning, Russell. Good morning, Vi,' said Mr Sprout softly at the door. 'Geography essays, please.'

Vi gasped when she saw the state of Mr Sprout. He was pale and stubbly and his normally neat hair was a mess. It looked like a bedhead, but the huge bags beneath Mr Sprout's eyes suggested that he hadn't been to bed at all. He looked awful.

She handed over the immaculate essay with more than a slight pang of guilt. Lying to Mr Sprout felt like kicking a kitten.

'Morning, sir,' said Sally sweetly, handing over

her essay. 'Love what you're doing with your hair. Shabby chic is soooo in . . .'

'Thank you, Sally,' said Mr Sprout as Sally pulled a mean face behind his back. The class sniggered. Vi shuffled to the desk she shared with Russell.

'Right, first, a reminder that I will need your permission slips for Wednesday's class trip to Dulworth Cove by tomorrow morning,' Mr Sprout began.

Vi tried not to moan. She bet the field trips at Rimmington Hall were more exciting than some stupid cove. She *had* to get into that school.

'Now, before we proceed with this morning's Spanish lesson, let's firm up our learning on coastal erosion. Please turn to page seventy-two of your textbooks and complete the quiz while I look over your essays.'

The class groaned.

'In silence, please,' Mr Sprout added, picking an essay out of the pile.

Vi looked at the quiz. She had no idea what any of it meant…

'What's . . . hydraulic action?' Vi whispered as noiselessly as she could to Russell.

'You've just done a whole essay on it,' Russell whispered back, whizzing through the questions in front of him.

Vi's heart sank. She hadn't even looked at the essay, she'd just let her dad download it. She suddenly thought of the new phone in her bag. If she could just 'research' the answers . . .

She reached gently under the desk and grabbed her rucksack. Her light fingers were well practised at getting somewhere they shouldn't, so she quickly unzipped the bag and found the phone inside. She felt around the top where she had seen the power switch, and flicked the button on. She saw the phone light up in her bag.

'Valentine,' she heard Mr Sprout say, a grave look on his face. 'Can you come here, please?'

Uh oh.

She dropped the phone back in the bag and made her way to the front of the class.

'Here comes the bridesmaid. Not,' whispered Sally as she passed. Vi 'accidentally' banged into her desk.

'Yes . . . sir?' she said as Mr Sprout looked at her intently.

'Valentine,' he whispered slowly. 'I'm going to

give you one chance to own up. Is there anything you want to tell me?'

Vi thought about the phone in her bag. How did he know? Would he tell Mum? She shook her head. Saying nothing was the only safe option right now.

'OK,' said Mr Sprout, picking up her essay. 'In which case, could you please explain the process of attrition?'

'Er . . . well . . . don't you know?' she blustered. 'Because you really should . . .'

'I see,' said Mr Sprout. 'Then tell me more about the Zandmotor project in South Holland? You seem to have strong views about replicating it on the Norfolk coastline.'

'I . . . um . . .' said Valentine over the hum of her own panic.

'You'll have to help me with the last bit,' said Mr Sprout. 'Perhaps you could translate the quote you cited from the poet Aeschylus? Because you've written it in Ancient Greek.'

'Pffff – it's all Greek to me, sir,' she laughed nervously.

'Vi, I know you didn't do this homework,' Mr Sprout whispered.

'You don't know that,' said Vi defensively.

'Yes, I do,' said Mr Sprout gently. 'For one thing, I know you struggle with geography. You once told me that the capital of Zambia was the letter Z.'

Vi shrugged. Wasn't it?

'And for another,' Mr Sprout continued, turning the second page around for her to see, 'you left the links in from where you downloaded this from the internet. There is more chance of Norfolk moving to Lusaka – which by the way is *actually* the capital of Zambia – than of you having written this. I know things are . . . challenging at the moment, but I'm incredibly disappointed, both as your teacher and as . . .'

'As what?' Vi asked. Was he still her nearly-stepfather? Were he and Easter still together? Did he even know what was going on?

'As someone who cares about you. Very much,' whispered Mr Sprout.

Vi slowly exhaled. That was a low blow.

'You leave me no choice,' said Mr Sprout, putting the essay back down on the pile. 'I will have to report this to Mrs Hasan and . . . and your mother. Sit down – we'll deal with it later.'

Vi trudged back to her desk with a heavy heart. Her mum was going to eliminate her when she heard about this.

'OK, textbooks closed, let's practise our Spanish,' Mr Sprout began. 'Who wants to read out the commands you researched in our last lesson? Anyone?'

Sally's hand shot up.

'Valentine wants to,' said Sally with a saccharine grin. 'She told me.'

Vi shot Sally a dirty look. She was such a snake.

'Excellent,' said Mr Sprout. 'Start us off, please, Vi.'

Vi pulled out her Spanish notebook.

'*¡Baila como un pollo!*' she read out loud.

'Great,' said Mr Sprout, writing it on the board. 'What does it mean?'

'It means,' Vi grinned, 'dance like a chicken!'

Mr Sprout dropped his board marker and the class sniggered. But rather than pick it up, Mr Sprout bent his arms at the elbows, bent his knees and started clucking rhythmically as he danced around the room.

'Er . . . sir?' asked Tom with a smirk. 'Are you OK?'

'A little tired, but fine, thank you, Tom,' said Mr Sprout calmly, still chicken-dancing around the room. 'Let's have another one, Vi.'

'Er, *¡coma la mesa!*' Vi said. 'It means, eat the . . .'

Before she could finish, Mr Sprout dropped to his knees and started hungrily gnawing at the table. The class let out a couple of shocked laughs.

'Vi! Give him another one!' Sally said excitedly. 'This is hilarious!'

'Don't do it,' whispered Russell. 'Something's not right.'

'Do it!' Sally egged on, looking at Vi in a way that made her feel cool for the first time ever.

Vi watched her nearly-stepfather chewing on the table. What was he doing?

'Come on, Vi,' her classmates started whispering. 'Do it!'

Vi looked back at her book. Was this what it was like to be popular? It felt really good . . .

'Um . . . *¡canta como un mono!*' she shouted out gleefully as Mr Sprout began to make strange noises. 'Sing like a monkey!'

'Vi – stop it,' Russell repeated as his father belted out some opera, monkey-style.

The class was helpless with laughter as Vi read

through her homework – *¡mueve el trasero!* (wiggle your bottom!); *¡haz malabarismos con tus lápices!* (juggle your pencils!); *¡salta como una rana!* (jump like a frog!).

'Go, Vi! Go, Vi! Go, Vi!' Year Six chanted through their hysterical giggles as she called command after command. Vi was high on their cheers. She was giddy with their popularity, she was—

'What on EARTH is going on here?' Mrs Hasan shouted from the doorway.

She was in so much trouble.

'Stop this at ONCE!' the head teacher boomed, bringing Mr Sprout back to his feet, where he picked up his board marker and continued as if nothing had happened. Vi quickly turned her phone off in her bag. You were supposed to hand your phones in at the start of the day. If she was caught with hers, she'd lose it for sure.

'What is going on?' Mrs Hasan demanded again. Her black hair was always pulled off her brown face, making her look business-like on a good day, and very stern on a bad one. A red bindi sat between her eyebrows. And her eyebrows weren't happy. Mrs Hasan was fair, but she was firm. And Vi knew she was about to be reminded just how firm.

'It was Vi,' said Sally, pointing to Vi like the viper she was. 'And she's got a phone in her bag. I just saw her switch it off.'

'Is this true, Valentine?' Mrs Hasan asked as Vi tried to slip her hand back into her bag, just as Russell kicked it with his feet. 'Kindly keep your hands where I can see them.'

'Um . . . Valentine doesn't own a phone,' said Mr Sprout. 'Susan – her mother – won't allow it.'

'Then she won't mind me looking in her bag,' Mrs Hasan said, summoning Vi to the front. 'Bring it here, please, Ms Day.'

Vi tried not to wince. Now she was in even more trouble. Russell handed her the bag and Vi walked it slowly to the front, delivering it to Mrs Hasan's outstretched arms. She watched as Mrs Hasan rummaged through it. Any second now, the phone would be discovered and she'd be . . .

'Sally,' said Mrs Hasan. 'Before you make accusations, I'll thank you to check your facts.'

'But . . . but . . . she did, miss, I saw it . . .' Sally blithered.

'Enough,' said Mrs Hasan, raising her hand.

'Thank you, Vi. I'm sorry for doubting you.'

Vi breathed a silent sigh of relief. She'd got away with it.

'Mrs Hasan,' Mr Sprout said sadly, picking up Vi's essay. 'I'm glad you're here, there's something I need to discuss with you.'

Or not.

Vi took her bag and went back to her desk. She felt around inside. The phone had gone. But where?

She felt a gentle nudge from Russell, who pointed to his left trouser pocket. There was her phone. He'd saved her. But why?

She watched as Mr Sprout whispered into Mrs Hasan's ear. Vi felt the head teacher's steely gaze light on her.

'I see,' said Mrs Hasan as Vi felt her stomach lurch. 'Valentine Day? I think you'd better come with me.'

After a thorough interrogation from Mrs Hasan, when Vi had to admit to cheating on her homework, Vi was sitting in the office trying not to cry.

As soon as the school secretary came in, she'd call Easter and then Valentine might as well cancel her life until she was fifty.

But instead of Mrs Price, the usual school secretary, a stressed-out young white man – Vi guessed he was only in his twenties – came rushing into the office. He looked like his mum had dressed him in his dad's clothes, putting him in a V-neck jumper underneath a suit. His left hand kept nervously smoothing down his wet red hair.

'Right – you'll have to help me,' he panted. 'Mrs Price has been called away to care for her mother. I'm Mr Rogers, from the temp agency. Are you the one who threw up in PE?'

'Not today.'

'Banged your head on the monkey bars?'

'Nope – that was Zach Smith. He does it most days – his mum left pre-signed forms in the third drawer down under the first aid kit.'

'You have a hospital appointment to freeze your verrucas?'

'Eurgh – no,' Vi answered, watching Mary Blachford blush on the other side of the room. 'Mrs Hasan wanted you to call my . . .'

'. . . parents, that's it,' he said, going to his

computer and typing in a password. 'Oh no! I've forgotten it again! I'm sure it was the name of her cat. Or her husband. Or her cat's husband. Argh – now I'm locked out! All the numbers are on this computer, how can I—'

'You can call my dad,' said Vi, inspiration suddenly striking as she rummaged around in her bag for his card. 'Here you go.'

She handed the card over to the grateful temp. Robert had said he was always going to be there for her. Now was his chance to prove it.

Not ten minutes later, Robert's slick black sports car screeched into the school car park. Vi saw her dad wink at her as he strolled casually past.

'Mr Ford,' said Mrs Hasan sternly. 'Please follow me.'

Vi gulped. Mrs Hasan could be seriously ferocious when she wanted. She was a rock. She was a mountain. There was no way Dad could talk her out of this one.

But within fifteen minutes, a smiling – no, a giggling – Mrs Hasan emerged from her office, her long black hair flowing around her shoulders and her eyebrows now dancing happily at Robert's flirtatious smile.

'You can't possibly mean that,' she said, patting her hair. 'I look older than the hills.'

'The hills of beauty, then,' said Robert smoothly, kissing her hand. Vi's jaw scraped the carpet. No one kissed Mrs Hasan. Probably not even Mr Hasan.

'And thank you so much for giving Vi the afternoon off. I'm sure this meeting will help her to become the kind of citizen of which Norton-on-Sea Primary is so rightfully proud.'

'It's no trouble at all,' beamed Mrs Hasan. 'I'm so sorry to have called you out here for a misunderstanding.'

'*De rien*,' winked Robert. '*Au revoir* . . . or I hope, *à bientôt* . . . Come along, Valentine.'

Vi watched her strict head teacher wave coyly at her father as they headed to the car. Only when they were safely inside did she dare to open her mouth.

'How . . . what . . . That was . . .' she gabbled. 'How did you *do* that?'

'Never reveal your methods,' Robert winked.

'But it is said that charm is the most effective weapon of all. Well, apart from a tank, but I'm glad it didn't come to that. Now come with me. I have a few people I'd like you to meet.'

CHAPTER 8

'So, where are we going?' Vi belched happily, after a big lunch at Burger World.

'To my support group,' said Robert. 'You said you'd be my sponsor, remember?'

'Oh yeah,' said Vi distractedly.

'Something on your mind?' Robert asked.

In truth, there was. The visit from SPIDER the previous day had Vi confused. If Umbra really was back, why had Robert kept it from her? Did he not know? Or was he actually working for Umbra? Was her father still a super-villain? She decided to investigate subtly.

'Are you still working for Umbra as a super-villain?' she asked.

Robert swerved the car. It was the first time he'd lost his cool, Vi noted.

'What? Why . . . Umbra's been dead for years,' Robert stammered.

Lie.

'Some people don't think so,' said Vi.

'Like who?' Robert asked. 'Where did you hear that?'

'Never reveal your methods,' winked Vi. 'But you haven't answered my question. Are you still working for Umbra?'

'What . . . why would you ask me that?'

'You asked me to be your sponsor, to keep you on the straight and narrow,' Vi replied. 'And you're answering a question with a question. That usually means someone is avoiding the truth.'

Robert pulled the car over. Vi suddenly felt nervous. Had she said too much?

'Valentine,' said Robert, taking his hand in hers and looking her squarely in the eye. 'I will only say this once. You have my word. I am no longer working for Umbra. I swear it.'

No stammer. Vi scrutinized her father's face. He looked like he was telling the truth. But what about the Neurotrol and the power station? Did he know about those? She wanted to ask. Although if Robert really was bad, asking him more would compromise SPIDER's operation . . . Being a spy was complicated.

'What's Umbra like?' Vi asked. 'Is he . . . she . . . Is Umbra a he or a she?'

'No one knows,' Robert shrugged. 'Umbra never came out of the shadows. No one knew who Umbra was. Even me. I never saw Umbra's face.'

'Really?' said Vi.

'Really,' said Robert still without a trace of stammer, restarting the car. 'Like I say – Umbra stayed in the shadows. And if Umbra is still alive, that's how . . . While we're being so honest, you don't happen to know what happened to that old phone you found yesterday?'

Vi's heart quickened. Busted.

'What old phone?' she said airily.

'Answering a question with a question,' murmured Robert. 'That usually means someone is avoiding the truth.'

Vi held her father's gaze and hoped that it wasn't betraying her trembling innards.

'I don't have it,' she said honestly. After all, it was still sitting in Russell's trouser pocket.

'I see,' said Robert. 'Well, someone has stolen it. It takes a thief to know a thief. And it's very important I get it back.'

'Why?' asked Vi. 'You said it was an old phone.'

'It . . . it doesn't belong to me,' Robert stammered. 'And the owner wants it.'

That didn't make sense. Robert had said the phone was going to be recycled. Vi went to get her water bottle out of her rucksack, the car suddenly felt very warm . . . that was weird. The zip was closed. She never closed the zip – it kept breaking, so she always left her bag partly open. Someone had been in her bag. Someone was looking for something. And that same someone was looking at her now.

'That phone is very important to me,' said Robert. 'If you know where it is, you need to tell me, Vi. Do you have it?'

Vi considered her options. This was a difficult choice. If she came clean to her dad, perhaps he wouldn't want to see her any more. Plus he still might be an evil criminal mastermind and have her eliminated. Plus she wouldn't have a phone any more. If she said nothing, none of those things would happen.

Actually, that was an easier choice than she thought.

'I don't have it,' she repeated again.

Robert pursed his lips.

'Well, if you come across it,' he said, 'you need to tell me. I mean it, Vi. I need it back.'

'OK,' said Vi as they pulled up outside a small green hall in the car park of St Xavier's, the Norton-on-Sea parish church. 'Now, let's get to this group of yours.'

She jumped out of the car before Robert could say anything more. She let out the breath she didn't realize she'd been holding. That was close. Too close.

They walked through the car park and into the dimly lit church hall. Vi noted the wooden stage, a few chairs dotted around and a tea urn boiling away on a trestle table. In fact, there was only one slight difference between this and any other church hall Vi had visited.

This one had a vampire, a clown and a scientist with two heads sitting in the middle of it.

Vi froze to the spot.

'Hi everyone,' said Robert, putting an encouraging hand on Vi's back. 'Sorry I'm late, I was collecting my daughter. Everyone, this is Vi.'

'Hi Vi,' came the cheery response from the

bizarre group.

'Allow me to introduce you,' Robert said, gesturing first to the vampire, who was sitting with a bat on the right shoulder of his black cape. 'This is Dimitri – formerly the Terror of Transylvania, lately the Teaching Assistant of Torquay.'

'A pleasure to meet you,' said Dimitri in a thick accent that reminded Vi of a cartoon vampire she used to watch on TV. 'How would you prefer I greet you? Would you like to shake hands, high-five, or perhaps simply exchange a verbal greeting? I'm conscious that as an older man of Caucasian heritage, I have enjoyed a privilege that mustn't compel you to greet me in a way that conflicts with any cultural or religious sensitivities, nor impose on your empowered womanhood.'

Vi nodded as if she'd understood even the smallest percentage of what Dimitri had just said.

'Er, hi,' she said, giving a small wave. Dimitri simply bowed slightly. But unless she was very much mistaken, the bat waved back with a small squeak.

'Nigel!' said Dimitri firmly. 'Don't you think women have had men speak for them for long enough without you batsplaining to our young sister, here? Respect her voice!'

Nigel squeaked back at Dimitri. Vi didn't speak any Bat, but she didn't get the impression that Nigel was respecting Dimitri's voice.

'And this,' said Robert, gesturing to the two-headed scientist, 'is . . .'

'. . . the proof that two heads ain't always better than one!' cried the left head, which was white and covered in a shock of green hair.

'Will you be quiet?' snapped the right-hand head, which was green and covered in a shock of white hair. 'Hello Valentine, I—'

'*We*,' corrected the left head.

'*We*,' sighed the scientist, 'are Dr Doppelganger. It's our pleasure to meet you.'

'Um . . . hello,' said Valentine, not sure which head to talk to. 'Nice to meet you. Both.'

'I'm sorry if my appearance alarms you,' said Dr Doppelganger's right head. 'I am—'

'*We* are,' the left head corrected again.

'*We are*,' the right head continued, 'the product of a freak accident. I was working late in the lab one night . . .'

'Ha!' laughed the left. 'Working?'

'I *was* working,' said the right head. 'I was

working in the lab . . .'

'Yuh-huh,' his left head mocked, 'as the cleaner!'

'It doesn't matter what I was doing there,' huffed the right. 'I was working in the lab late one night, when I knocked over a toxic substance and a freak chemical reaction occurred.'

'Ha – you knocked over some toilet cleaner with your mop,' scoffed his left head. 'You had an allergic reaction. You're not a mad scientist. You're a bad scientist.'

'Will you BE QUIET?' roared the right head. 'I'm trying to explain how Dr Doppelganger was born—'

'And that's another thing,' his left head interrupted. 'He's not even a real doctor.'

'Yes, I am!' snapped the right head defensively. 'I have a PhD! I got a distinction!'

'In Peruvian Folk Music from University.com,' mocked the left. 'You downloaded your doctorate from the internet!'

'*Bonjour, mademoiselle*!' screeched a very French voice in Vi's right ear. '*Je suis* Auguste, I am delighted to make *votre* acquaintance.'

Vi turned to see the clown grinning wildly in

her face. Auguste was smothered in white paint, with messy triangular eyebrows and a smudged red mouth. She felt Robert's arm go protectively around her shoulders. Clowns freaked her out. Especially this one.

'Oh . . . hey,' she said, shaking the clown's oversized gloved hand.

'Please, smell *ma fleur*,' said Auguste, proffering the huge red plastic flower on his green dungarees.

'Er, no, thank you, Auguste,' said Robert, laughing nervously and moving Vi gently away. 'We all know that old chestnut! If Vi smells your flower, you'll squirt her with water and she'll get all wet.'

'*Non, non, non* – zis is *ridicule*!' said Auguste seriously. 'I would never do such a silly thing to zees lovely little girl.'

'Well done, Auguste,' said Dimitri. 'This demonstrates real growth from you.'

'*Merci*,' said Auguste with a small bow. '*Non* – if anyone smells zees flower, I will squirt zem with deadly poison and zey will die a slow, 'orrible death! Zis is a funny joke, *non*?'

Auguste fell about laughing wildly. No one else did.

'You bring whole new levels of meaning to

"toxic masculinity",' muttered Dimitri.

'So sorry, everyone,' puffed a middle-aged white woman with masses of messy brown curls, bursting into the room wearing a lanyard identifying her as Sandra. 'My other Ex-Villain Improvement League group made me late again. Those guys will be the death of me.'

'Big talkers, huh?' said the left head as Dr Doppelganger took his seat alongside the other group members. Robert gestured towards two chairs for him and Vi.

'No,' said Sandra with a bright smile. 'I mean they are literally trying to kill me. I've just had to run for my life. Third time this week. Occupational hazard. Anyway, let's start with our pledge.'

Vi watched as they all stood up and put a hand to heart. She listened as they spoke together:

'We solemnly swear to do our best
And stay on the path of virtue
Renounce our evil, wicked ways
And not use piranhas to hurt you.'

'Grrrrreat,' said Sandra, sitting down and pushing her hair out of her face. 'So, it's fantastic to see you again and just wonderful that some of your sponsors could join us today. Um . . . Auguste?'

'*Oui*,' said Auguste innocently, looking at the ceiling.

'Where is your sponsor?' said Sandra gently.

'Er . . . he . . . he was ill,' said Auguste guiltily.

'Auguste,' Sandra coaxed. 'We've talked about this. I can't help you unless you respect the honesty of this space. Where is your sponsor?'

Auguste rolled his eyes and slumped in his chair.

'It is not *ma faute*,' he said, running his hands through his green hair. 'He couldn't take a joke. I had to let him go.'

'Let him go?' Sandra asked.

'From ze top of a cliff,' grinned Auguste. 'Zis is a funny joke, *non*?'

'Sure – I bet it killed him,' said Dr D's left head as Auguste laughed maniacally.

'Auguste – that's the fifth sponsor you've . . . let go this month,' said Sandra. 'If you're going to stay in this programme, you need to find someone you can work with. Someone you trust. Someone who survives more than a week. Do you understand me?'

'*Bof,*' muttered Auguste under his breath.

'OK, then,' said Sandra. 'Robert, it looks like you have made a big step too.'

'Yes,' said Robert proudly. 'This is my daughter, Valentine. She's going to be my sponsor.'

'That's wonderful,' said Sandra as the group applauded. 'Valentine, you have been a major motivation for your father to leave villainy behind. It's wonderful to see you involved in his journey.'

Vi smiled at Robert. These people seemed convinced that her dad was making the right choices. Perhaps she should be too.

'So let's get on to this week's discussion, "Life Beyond the Lair: How to Get on the Property Ladder with No Volcano as a Deposit". To start us off . . .'

A low saxophone tune started playing at the door. There, standing in the half-light of the doorway, was a beautiful blonde woman, whose golden tresses perfectly framed her heart-shaped face. A tight red dress hugged her body, a black stole was draped casually around her pale white shoulders. Her long cigarette holder exhaled smoke rings, which floated over her body until they evaporated around her black high heels.

'Hi,' she said, not so much talking as exhaling. 'Room for a small one?'

'Lady,' said Dr Doppelganger's left head, as she slunk across the room, her high heels ringing out like pistol shots. 'How'd you like to get our heads together sometime?'

'That is so objectifying,' scoffed Dimitri as Nigel let out a bat whistle on his shoulder.

'Siren,' said Robert, standing to greet the new arrival with a kiss on her hand. 'Long time no see. Still as breathtaking as ever.'

'You'll have to forgive me for being late,' Siren pouted, exhaling a kiss-shaped smoke ring as she sat down and crossed her long legs.

'Was it the long fall from heaven?' the doctor's left head asked.

'No,' breathed Siren, shaking her golden hair as the saxophone music played on. 'I had black bean and lentil stew for lunch. My farts could kill a dog.'

'I . . . applaud your truth,' whispered Dimitri uncertainly, moving his chair away.

'I'm ever so sorry,' whispered Sandra, 'but you can't smoke in here. And would you mind awfully asking your friend to stop playing his saxophone? We're trying to have a little chat.'

'Sure thing, sister,' breathed Siren, switching her e-cigarette off. 'Dave's my sponsor. And my soundtrack. Dave – take five.'

Dave tipped his hat coolly and put his saxophone in his lap.

'I hope you don't mind me butting in,' said Siren. 'But I want to go straight.'

Vi heard Auguste chuckle on the other side of the room.

'Something funny, Bobo?' Siren breathed angrily, fixing Auguste with a piercing stare.

'Forgive me – I'm just *un petit peu* surprised,' said Auguste. 'You are ze greatest femme fatale of all time. You have ze world at your 'igh-'eeled feet. Why would you give it up?'

'I've had enough of the inequality,' Siren pouted. 'Did you know that female super-villains earn on average fifteen per cent less from ransom, extortion and blackmail than their male counterparts? I'm sick of trying to break through the glass ceiling.'

'The patriarchy has a lot to answer for,' Dimitri sighed.

'So does security at the Louvre,' said Siren. 'Seriously, I've tried to break through that glass ceiling to steal *The Mona Lisa* five times now. No, I am a new woman.'

'I like the old one,' said Dr Doppelganger's left head, earning him a headbutt from the right.

Sandra's phone bleeped.

'Oh no – I am so sorry,' she said, reading her text. 'I'm going to have to cut this short. I need to go and rescue a co-worker so she can pick up her kids.'

'Overwhelmed by the unreasonable expectations on working parents?' Dimitri asked.

'No, she's being held hostage by the Former Criminal Overlord Society,' smiled Sandra. 'Such rewarding work. Now, Siren, before you can join our group, you need to earn your New Leaf Badge. We need to see evidence of your rehabilitation before we can support you. You see – everyone has one.'

Vi noted the small golden leaves on everyone's clothes. She hoped her dad had earned his rather than stolen it.

'I'll lay off the lentils, if you like,' breathed Siren, elevating her left side.

'I'm afraid it'll take a little more than that,' said Sandra, holding her nose as she stood up. 'Although it would be an excellent start. No, you need to demonstrate that you are actively working for good, as witnessed by a sponsor in this group. Otherwise, I'm afraid you're on your own. I'll see you all next week. Be good. And if you can't be good . . .'

'. . . you'll go to prison,' chimed the group as Sandra rushed out of the door, calling pleasantly for police back-up as she went.

Siren slumped in her chair.

'What's a girl got to do to be good?' she sulked.

'*Peut-être* you could carry ze air freshener?' sniffed Auguste.

'Come along, Vi, we'd better get you back to school before your mother gets there,' said Robert.

Vi looked at the grumpy Siren. An inspired idea suddenly struck her.

It takes a thief to know a thief, Robert had said.

Siren was a master thief who needed a New Leaf Badge to get into the group. Vi was a hopeful spy who needed the Neurotrol to get into Rimmington Hall. She could sense an alliance . . .

'Er – I'll meet you in the car,' Vi said to Robert. 'I just need the loo.'

'I'd give it five minutes if I were you,' warned Siren.

'Um,' said Robert uncertainly, looking at Auguste. 'I'm not sure if I should leave.'

'Don't sweat it, Robbie,' winked Siren. 'I'll keep an eye on her. We girls gotta stick together.'

'OK,' said Robert. 'I need to make a call anyway. Don't be too long, Vi.'

He walked out of the hall, followed by Dimitri, Auguste and Dr Doppelganger. Vi counted to ten to make sure they weren't coming back, then sat on the chair next to Siren.

'Erm, Siren?' she said.

'Hey kiddo,' said Siren. 'What can I do for you?'

'Well – it's more what we could do for each other,' said Vi. 'You need your New Leaf Badge. I need some help to do good.'

'I'm listening,' said Siren.

'I'm trying to find someone. A thief,' said Vi. 'Do you know Frankie the Fence? I need to find something that's been stolen, something important . . .'

'Then you can bet your bottom dollar that Frankie's had a hand in it,' smiled Siren. 'And that he's just stolen your bottom dollar.'

Vi's heart quickened. A lead – at last.

'Could you take me to him?' she asked. 'I'm trying to stop Umbra. If you help me, I'll nominate you and then you can get your New Leaf Badge . . .'

Siren looked long and hard at Vi.

'Is it OK with your dad?' she said.

Vi thought quickly. If she was going to be a spy, she was going to have to tell the occasional lie . . .

'Sure,' she said. 'He's just too shy to ask you himself. I think he has a bit of a crush on you.'

'Does he now?' said Siren with an amused smile. 'OK, kiddo. Meet me tomorrow at 3.30 p.m. at the amusement arcade on the end of Norton Pier. I'll take you to Frankie.'

Vi grinned. Mission accomplished.

They headed outside, where Robert was on the phone in his car.

'Really good to meet you, Siren,' smiled Vi.

'You too, kiddo,' Siren winked back, sashaying past Robert. 'Now, if you'll excuse me, I have to slip into something more . . . comfortable.'

Vi watched as Robert accepted the kiss Siren blew at him with a smile.

'Seriously,' said the super-villainess. 'These pants are giving me an epic wedgie.'

Umbra was tiring of unwelcome phone conversations.

'I warned you, Robert,' Umbra growled down the phone. 'And it's very rare I give warnings . . .'

'I'm telling you, I'll get it,' Robert insisted. 'Just give me a little more time. If you could wait another few days . . .'

'I'm done with waiting!' Umbra shouted. 'Ten years I have waited in the shadows! And you have the audacity to tell me to wait a few more days!'

'I'm sorry,' said Robert quickly.

'You should be,' sighed Umbra impatiently. 'I told you that if you couldn't deal with this situation, then I would. And it will be dealt with. Today.'

There was a silence. Robert was thinking. Umbra didn't pay Robert to think.

'When you contacted me six months ago,' Robert began, 'when you let me know you were still alive and had new plans, we made a deal: I would give you the Neurotrol and I would give you Easter. And in return, you would give me a huge amount of money so I could retire. The girl was never part of the plan.'

'Well, the moment she stole my Neurotrol, she made herself part of the plan. I told you, Robert – there is no place for sentimentality in my organization,' Umbra said. 'You told me that the girl was merely a means for you to get to Easter Day, so you could deliver my arch-nemesis to me when I was ready to take my revenge. You're not going soft on me, are you? Because if I think for one moment that you are . . .'

'No,' said Robert. 'Of course not. You do what you have to do. Vi . . . Valentine . . . the girl . . . she means nothing.'

'Glad to hear it,' said Umbra, glancing over at the disguise that had been unused and unnecessary for nearly a decade. 'Because it is nearly time. Bring Easter Day to the power station on

Wednesday night. I will take care of the Neurotrol myself. And unless Valentine Day moves out of my way, she's going to discover just how unsentimental I can be.'

CHAPTER 9

'WHERE HAVE YOU BEEN?' Easter raged as they screeched up outside the school. 'I've been going out of my mind!'

Easter pulled her daughter protectively into her arms. Even with her face buried in the massive hug, Vi could practically feel the steam coming off her mother. This was going to get ugly.

'Mum – chill – I was with Robert,' Vi said, squished against her mum, not really expecting that fact to help. 'The school knew . . .'

'Well, I didn't!' yelled Easter, looking directly at Robert. 'I had no idea where you were – that office temp told me you were having your tonsils out. I thought . . . I thought . . . Urgh, Valentine, I will deal with you later. Right now I need to talk to your father. Get in the car!'

'It's my fault,' said Vi, not wanting to get her dad into any more trouble. 'Don't be angry with him.'

'Too. Late,' glowered Easter. 'I said I will deal with you later. Get in the car, Valentine. Now.'

Vi knew better than to argue with her mother when she was in this mood. She gave her dad an apologetic look, which was returned with a friendly wink. He was smiling now. She doubted he would be by the time Mum finished with him.

Vi got in the car and shut the door behind her. Barely had it closed before her mum started up.

'WHAT DID YOU THINK YOU WERE DOING TAKING MY DAUGHTER OUT OF SCHOOL?'

'She's my daughter too, Bunny,' Robert replied calmly.

'Now she is,' Easter raged. 'But for the past ten years, she's been my daughter. Just mine. The only person standing between her and all our enemies.'

'You're paranoid,' Robert scoffed.

'Maybe,' Easter hissed. 'But that paranoia has kept her safe. Unlike you . . .'

Vi slumped in her seat and tried not to listen as her parents fought in the school car park.

'Your mum's been freaking out,' said a small voice from the back of the car. 'She was really scared.'

Vi turned around and scowled at Russell.

'I was with my dad,' she snarled.

'A notorious super-villain,' said Russell. 'You can't blame her for stressing.'

'Yes, I can,' snapped Vi. 'Stay out of things you don't know.'

She crossed her arms to signal that the conversation was over.

'I know about this,' said Russell, carefully slipping her phone between the seats. Vi had forgotten about that. She should really thank Russell for getting her out of trouble.

But she didn't.

The argument between her mum and dad was getting louder outside. Easter's voice was now so high only dogs could hear it. Her dad's pitch didn't change, but his volume did.

'You can't keep her wrapped in cotton wool!' he shouted. 'You can't always protect her from everything and everyone! She needs to learn how to protect herself!'

Easter opened the door a chink, allowing Vi to

hear her parting shot more clearly than she wanted to.

'Well, I can protect her from you,' she promised, before getting in her seat and slamming the door.

'Seat belt on!' she ordered as she turned the key in the ignition. 'Now!'

'By the way,' Robert shouted outside the car. 'Your bum always *did* look big in that leather catsuit! I LIED!'

Easter put her foot on the accelerator and roared into the road.

Valentine wanted to get cross with her mum but realized a) there was no point, and b) she didn't really have the right. She knew how protective Mum was. And – irritatingly – Russell was right. When Easter arrived at the school and Vi wasn't there, it would have confirmed her worst fears. She must have been terrified.

They drove home in stony silence.

'You're late,' said Indy as Easter stomped into the house. 'I was about to send out a rescue squad.'

'Don't get me started,' growled Easter. 'Valentine – go upstairs and get changed. Nan wants you to take her to Autumn Leaves. When you get back, we'll talk about you cheating on your homework.'

'But—' Valentine began.

'Valentine!' Mum snapped. 'Upstairs! Now!'

Vi trudged halfway up the stairs, then stopped to do some surveillance of what was being said in the kitchen.

'What happened?' she heard Nan ask.

'Robert,' said Easter darkly. Vi listened as her mum gave her version of events, which involved three calls to the police, two hospitals and someone called Harry the Hitman, who Vi hoped was a personal trainer. Her mum had clearly been terrified. Vi felt a pang of guilt spike her guts.

'I mean,' she said, almost out of breath from her angry tirade, 'can you believe that man? Can you believe him? Can you? CAN YOU?'

Nan said nothing. In Valentine's experience, this was a very dangerous move. The only safe answer in this situation was 'no'. But Nan rarely played safe.

'I understand why you're upset,' she said levelly. 'Robert was wrong to collect her without consulting you. I don't know if I've mentioned it, but the man's a complete idiot ...'

There was a 'but' coming.

'Don't do it, Nan,' Vi whispered. 'Don't do it.'

'But,' Nan continued, 'at least he's trying.'

There was a deathly silence.

'What did you say?' Easter whispered, as deadly as a snake hiss.

'I mean . . . while he went TOTALLY the wrong way about it,' Nan continued, 'at least he's trying to build some kind of relationship with Valentine. I mean, look at Genevieve.'

'This has nothing to do with Russell's mother,' hissed Easter again.

'Of course not,' said Nan soothingly. 'I'm just saying . . .'

'Well, don't!' snapped Easter. 'I don't want you to "just say"! She's my daughter and—'

'She's going to want a relationship with her father,' said Nan. 'Whether you like it or not. This isn't about you and him. This is about him and Valentine. You're going to need to find a way through this. For her sake.'

'I love my girl more than life itself,' said Easter firmly. 'I have spent every waking minute keeping Vi safe. I'm not going to endanger all that now. Tomorrow I call the lawyers. I need to keep Robert away.'

'But if you go to court, your whole past will come out. What about George?' said Nan.

'What about him?' said Easter bitterly. 'I don't even know if he's going to stay. But Vi will. And I need to keep her safe. I tried to be reasonable, but Robert has stepped over the mark. This is war.'

Vi walked slowly up to her bedroom. She'd heard enough.

And yet she knew that this wasn't the last she would hear of it. Not by a million miles.

'It'll all get figured out,' said Nan as they walked towards the Autumn Leaves that evening. 'Easter and George, Easter and Robert – they'll find their way. Don't you worry.'

Vi sighed.

'Were they ever happy?' she asked.

'Your parents?' asked Nan. 'Oh, they thought they were. When your mum told me that she'd run off with Sir Charge and you were on the way, she described them as "dynamite".'

'So what happened?' asked Vi, instinctively turning her head. She thought she'd heard someone behind her . . .

'Exactly what happens to dynamite,' smiled Nan. 'It exploded. Robert was never the right man for your mother – and not just because he was Sir Charge. She needs ice to her fire. She needs someone calm, someone dependable. Someone exactly like George Sprout.'

'Really?' Vi asked, checking behind her again. 'He's just so . . . ordinary.'

'Nothing wrong with ordinary,' said Nan. 'A spy's life throws up enough drama. You want ordinary at home. Your grandfather gave me that, God rest his soul. And George can give it to your mother.'

Vi was confident that life with a super-spy mother and super-villain father wasn't going to be ordinary. And she was also confident that someone was following them. But when she turned around again, there was no one there. She shook her head. The last thing she needed was Mum's paranoia rubbing off on her.

'They both love you – very much,' said Nan. 'That's why they're fighting so hard. You only battle this hard when you really care.'

'Just so long as they don't eliminate each other

while they're doing it,' Vi muttered.

'Ultimately, their missions have the same objective,' Nan promised. 'Just hide all the weaponry while they figure it out . . .'

Vi smiled as they walked up the steps to Autumn Leaves, Vi taking one last look at the empty space behind them before entering the red-brick, converted Victorian hospital. After Grandad died and Indy moved in with Vi and Easter, Indy wanted some like-minded company. Autumn Leaves was like a youth club for old people – they were constantly cooking or doing needlework or playing croquet. Indy had a room there and she stayed over a night or two a week to be with her friends – like a senior citizens' sleepover.

They walked into the glass-ceilinged recreation room, where several of Nan's friends were dotted around. Vi recognized an elderly white couple – Desmond, who was building a model aeroplane from matchsticks, and his wife Felicity, who was sitting opposite him knitting.

'Can you pass me the glue?' Desmond asked his wife.

'WHAT?' Felicity shouted back. 'WHY

WOULD YOU ASK FOR A POO?'

Vi giggled. Despite being very hard of hearing, Felicity refused to wear the hearing aid that would make everyone's – especially Desmond's – life that little bit easier. And very much quieter.

Desmond sighed and reached over the table to pick up the glue. He waved it at Felicity to make his point.

'WELL, I DON'T THINK THAT'S GOING TO HELP YOU,' Felicity boomed, returning to her knitting, accidentally knocking Desmond's matchstick aeroplane and bringing the whole thing clattering down. 'OOOPS! YOU NEED TO PAY ATTENTION TO WHAT YOU'RE DOING, DES! I DON'T KNOW WHY YOU CAN'T CONCENTRATE!'

Nan sat down in an armchair.

'So,' she said, 'let's get you to Rimmington Hall. They can teach you everything you need to know.'

'Fighting, weapons, explosions,' Vi said enthusiastically.

'Thinking, protecting, staying alive,' Nan corrected. 'Spying is about keeping people safe, yourself included. But if you're going to find this

Neurotrol before Umbra, you're going to need some back-up.'

Nan looked behind her.

'Desmond?' she whispered. 'Is the coast clear?'

Desmond got up and went to the door. He turned the sign on the door to 'Nap Time!' and gently shut it.

'All clear,' he shouted back, returning to his chair.

'SMALL BEER?' Felicity yelled. 'GO ON, THEN!'

Nan flipped open the arm of her armchair to reveal a set of buttons inside. She pressed the top one and immediately the glass roof started to cover over with screens dotted with coordinates and surveillance maps. She pressed the next one down and her voice suddenly became magnified around the room.

'Agents,' she announced. 'We have a Code Crochet, this is not a drill, I repeat, this is not a drill. Stand by.'

Vi looked around agog as the elderly residents, who had been variously snoozing and doing arts and crafts suddenly leapt to their feet and started taking positions around the changing room. An elderly white lady who had been watching *Antiques Challenge* on the TV flipped the remote to reveal that the widescreen TV was in fact a huge computer screen.

'What the . . .' Vi said, as the same lady reached over to a box of Snakes and Ladders and pulled out the wireless keyboard inside. 'What is going on?'

'Welcome to the Silver Service,' said Nan proudly, gesturing around her. 'The elite spy division for the over-seventies.'

'But . . . but . . . you're all so . . .' Vi struggled to find the polite word.

'Experienced?' her nan suggested. 'I'm glad you think so. Unlike SPIDER. Or Stupid Protocol Indiscriminately Ditching Experienced Retirees, as we like to call it. That idiotic organization put us all out to pasture once we turned seventy. But it was ridiculous for our expertise to go to waste. So we formed our own unit. One of the advantages of age is that everyone assumes you don't know what's going on. We have branches all over the country.'

'Agent Labyrinth, I'm getting a report from Park Bench 439,' said the lady on the computer, squinting at the screen through silver half-moon glasses. 'They have detained the gang who were graffitiing the swings and have deployed a stern talking-to and a mint imperial incentive programme. The youths have seen the error of their ways and promise to visit their grandparents at least once a month.'

'Great work,' said Nan. 'Valentine, this is Wendy, Agent Pirate – one of the greatest technical whizzes of our age. There is nothing she can't hack and nothing she doesn't know. She can even FaceTime her grandson.'

'Pleasure to meet you, Veronica,' said Wendy, not taking her eyes off the screen.

'You just have to watch her memory,' Nan whispered. 'Not as sharp as it once was.'

'Hearing's fine, though,' said Wendy, tapping away at her computer.

Nan pulled an 'ooops' face.

Suddenly, there was a small explosion where Desmond and Felicity were sitting.

'SORRY!' yelled Felicity, waving away the smoke from a small explosive device that Desmond was tinkering with. 'DIDN'T MEAN TO DISTURB YOU!'

'You'll have to forgive my darling wife,' Desmond whispered to Vi. 'Years of being Agent Goliath, the greatest explosives expert in the world, did wonders to keep our world safe. It just wasn't so good for her hearing.'

'NONSENSE!' shouted Felicity. 'THERE'S NOTHING WRONG WITH MY STEERING!'

'What did you do when you were a . . . y'know?' Vi whispered to Desmond.

'Oh, this and that,' he said. 'I wasn't really cut out for the front line like your family. I was more backstage.'

'He's being absurdly modest,' Indy chipped in. 'Desmond – Agent Orb – is one of the greatest inventors in creation.'

'Not really,' said Desmond, blushing slightly. 'I just work on the principle: *If in doubt, blow it up.*'

'Agent Pirate,' Nan continued, turning her attention back to the giant computer. 'I need you to keep your ear out on the CobWeb.'

'The CobWeb?' Vi asked.

'The secret internet that the Silver Service uses to communicate,' Nan explained. 'It's everything we need: top secret, high speed, large font.'

'Right,' said Vi as Wendy's fingers raced

across the keys.

'I'm going to step out with Vi for some fresh air,' said Nan, returning to Wendy. 'Can you scan the web for any coded chat about Umbra or a Neurotrol?'

'Absolutely,' said Wendy, her fingers still flying across the keyboard. 'I'll run some BitLocker and PicoCrypt programmes. If those don't work, I'll run a frequency analysis and check for affine shift ciphers.'

'Sounds great,' said Indy. 'We'll leave you to it.'

'Ah – Agent Labyrinth, just one thing,' Wendy asked, turning to them.

'Anything you need,' said Nan.

'Can you remember me bloomin' password?'

CHAPTER 10

'How are *your* investigations going?' said Nan as they stepped out into the beautifully manicured gardens of Autumn Leaves.

'I've got a lead,' said Vi proudly. 'Frankie the Fence – Siren's taking me to him tomorrow to see what he knows about the Neurotrol.'

'Siren, eh?' said Nan. 'There's a blast from the past.'

'You know her?' Vi asked.

'Who doesn't?' said Nan. 'Just before I retired, she launched a daring attack on SPIDER HQ. My eyes still water at the memory.'

'She had tear gas?' asked Vi.

'She had wind,' said Nan. 'How are you mixed up with her?'

'She goes to the Ex-Villain Improvement

League,' Vi explained. 'Like my dad.'

'I see,' said Indy. 'Well, you be careful. Villains' habits die hard.'

'I will – Siren seems OK, though.'

'I wasn't just talking about Siren,' Nan warned as they rounded a pretty flowerbed. 'Now back to this Neurotrol. The first thing you need to find out is . . .'

Suddenly, as if from nowhere, Vi felt a hard shove on her back. She groaned and lurched forward, reaching out to break her fall. But before her arms could hit the ground, a hard tug wrenched her bag off her shoulder. Vi staggered to her feet just in time to see a figure swathed entirely in black sprinting away with her backpack.

'What the . . .' Vi gasped as the masked figure raced into the gardens. 'Stop! You – you give that back!'

Vi squinted at the thief, who was running towards the back gates. She couldn't see their face and a black cloak hid whether they were a man or a woman – but they were getting away. And fast. She went to sprint off after them, but felt a firm hand on her shoulder.

'Cool your jets – we need wheels,' said Nan,

scuttling towards an elderly lady sitting on a mobility scooter and giving her a shove into the flowerbed. 'Phyllis – I need to commandeer your vehicle.'

'Oi!' Phyllis shouted from the pansies as Nan straddled the mobility scooter and gestured for Vi to jump on the back. 'You can forget being my bridge partner next week!'

But Nan was already on the move, flooring the mobility scooter as fast as it would go.

Which, as it turned out, wasn't very fast.

'Er, Nan?' said Vi as they pootled along the gardens. 'Do you think we could speed up a bit?'

'Speed isn't everything,' said Nan, flipping open the speedometer on the front of the scooter. 'Just ask the tortoise.'

'The tortoise wasn't chasing a thief who's getting away with my bag!' Vi insisted as the crook disappeared out of sight around a corner.

'Trust me. They're not getting away,' said Nan, pressing the side of her glasses and releasing a small microphone from their left arm. 'This is Labyrinth paging Huntsman, come in, Huntsman.'

There was a crackle, but no reply.

'I repeat, come in, Huntsman – we have a

Tea Dance situation.'

Another crackle. More silence. Nan huffed.

'REG!' she yelled. 'I'm talking to you!'

'Oh, sorry,' came the voice on the other end of the line. 'I thought my code name was Crab?'

'No – that's Brian!' Nan shouted.

'Oh, hello Indy,' another voice piped up. 'Do you need anything from the shop? I'm going out for toffees.'

'Stand down, Brian!' Nan shouted. 'And that's negative on the toffees – last time you gummed up your dentures and were no use calling the bingo. Reg? Are you in position?'

'Affirmative,' Reg replied. 'I'm on the bench by the ornamental pond. By the way, did I tell you about my grandson's wedding? It was such a lovely day, you must see my slideshow.'

'Not now, Reg!' Nan shouted. 'Can you see the target?'

'Affirmative,' Reg repeated. 'Target approaching in T-minus ten seconds. Which reminds me, I'd love a nice cup of tea – I've got a lovely bit of Battenberg in my room.'

'REG – FOCUS!' said Nan, skidding around a corner.

'Reg – you have to stop the target!' Vi shouted, thinking of her new phone. 'They've got my . . . bag!'

'Roger that,' said Reg. 'Oh, how funny – my cousin knew a Roger once. I think he made curtains . . .'

'REG!!!' screamed Nan. 'Deploy delay tactics!'

'No need to shout,' huffed Reg, who Vi could now see was an elderly, bald white man in a cardigan and glasses, sitting on his bench with a bag of sweets.

'REG!' Vi shouted as the thief approached him. 'Do . . . whatever it is you're supposed to be doing!'

'All right,' huffed Reg, tipping his sweets all over the path. 'Whatever happened to the art of polite conversation?'

Vi watched as the small, round sweets bounced all over the path.

'What are those?' she asked her nan.

'Mint imperials,' smiled Nan as the thief started to skid and fall over the marble-like sweets. 'That should slow them down.'

It certainly did. The thief wobbled and teetered and struggled to stay upright as the little globes rolled under their feet.

'We're gaining!' cried Vi as the thief found their footing and stumbled off again. 'Get 'em, Nan!'

'Oh, we will,' promised Nan, revving the mobility scooter harder. 'Come in, White-Tail.'

'Is that you, Indy?' a lady's voice replied. 'You sound ever so funny on this gizmo.'

'Doris, are you in position?' Nan commanded.

'Affirmative,' Doris replied. 'I'm in the downward dog.'

'You're what?' said Nan. 'You're supposed to be by the herb garden!'

'Not on Mondays, dearie,' said Doris. 'It's bums, tums and hip replacements yoga in the physio room. You should give it a go, it's really firmed my bottom.'

'I'll firm your bottom with my FOOT!' shouted Nan in temper. 'Right, we'll have to do this ourselves.'

'Hurry up, Nan – they're getting away!' cried Vi, as the thief bolted towards the fence at the bottom of the gardens.

'No, they're not,' said Nan, flipping a switch on the handle. Immediately, the basket on the front of the scooter opened up, to reveal a large cannon.

The speedometer screen became a tracker, showing the thief running in and out of a large bullseye with the caption: *TARGET OUT OF RANGE.* 'Come on, come on . . .'

Nan waited until the thief was perfectly between the crosshairs. The screen changed to: *TARGET LOCKED.*

'Gotcha,' said Nan as she hit the red button, firing the cannon and sending the mobility scooter backwards with the force. Vi clung on to the back as she waited to see what fire power the scooter would emit . . .

But it wasn't a blast that came out of the cannon.

It was a long, knitted scarf.

'Take THAT!' yelled Nan as the scarf jetted through the air towards the thief. Vi watched it hurtle towards its target. 'We sew lead weights into the pom-poms. Works every time.'

Vi watched as the scarf curled through the air before reaching its target, wrapping itself around the runaway's legs and bringing them crashing to the ground.

'You did it!' cried Vi, rushing towards the thief as they desperately tried to untangle the scarf. As

Vi approached, she could finally see more of her attacker, who was dressed in something like black overalls, the kind she'd seen in martial arts movies, with a black cloak coming from a hooded mask over the thief's head. As she neared, she gasped as she saw their face – or lack of it. The mask took the form of a sheer, black, mirrored oval with a single mark etched on the front.

Two circles joined by intersecting lines. The darkest part of a shadow.

'Umbra,' she gasped.

'Step away, little girl,' a heavily disguised voice commanded. Vi stopped dead. The barrel of a gun was pointing at her. She could feel molten fear rushing through her veins. But she wasn't going to show it. 'You don't know what you're getting into.'

'Give me my bag,' said Vi shakily, trying to sound a lot braver than she felt.

'I'm not going to tell you again,' said Umbra, cocking the trigger. 'Step away before I . . . OW!'

The gun clattered to the floor as it was knocked from Umbra's hand by a large rock.

'What the—' Umbra shouted, instinctively grabbing the hurt hand and dropping Vi's bag.

'AND YOU CAN TAKE THAT!' roared Nan, coming up and thwacking Umbra with her handbag. 'HOW DARE YOU STEAL FROM MY GRANDAUGHTER, YOU WICKED, WICKED—'

Umbra rolled along the ground to avoid the blows, sprang up and started to sprint towards the back wall.

'Vi – stop!' Vi heard Nan call after her. But before she knew what she was doing, Vi took off in pursuit, propelled by a roar of courage – if she was quick, Umbra would be trapped by the high wall that ran along the back of the grounds. Vi ran as hard as she could, feeling a newly discovered thrill as she chased down her prey. They were approaching the wall – there was nowhere to go. Vi could catch Umbra. She could prove she was a spy. She could get into Rimmington Hall. She could . . .

She couldn't jump up a wall like Umbra could.

With the nimblest feet, the super-villain leapt up the wall like a parkour runner, placed their hands on the top and effortlessly vaulted over it. Vi ran to the wall and smacked it with her hand in frustration.

Umbra was gone. And now her hand hurt.

She walked back to where her backpack lay on the floor. She opened it. Phew! Her phone was still there.

Vi looked over at Nan, who was poking around in the bushes with her walking stick.

'Who threw that rock?' Vi asked. 'One of your friends?'

'No idea,' said Indy, shaking her head and heading back to the scooter. 'But you've got a guardian angel. We both owe them one. Are you OK?'

Vi jumped on the back of the mobility scooter. That was scary. But, wow, so exciting.

'I'm fine,' she sighed bravely.

'Good,' said Nan, smacking Vi's hand with her handbag.

'Ow!' moaned Vi. 'What was that for?'

'Don't ever be that stupid again,' Nan warned. 'Taking off unarmed after a super-villain who just held a gun at you . . .'

'Umbra dropped the gun!' Vi exclaimed.

'And might have had another four, for all you knew,' Nan said. 'Know your enemy. Umbra is dangerous. Good spies stay alive.'

Nan revved up the scooter and chuntered away

while Vi sulked on the back.

'What was that all about, anyway?' said Nan, as they approached the main building. 'I haven't seen a gun pulled that fast since last quiz night.'

'I'm not sure,' said Vi, holding her backpack. That was the second time today someone had wanted her bag – first Robert, now Umbra. But why?

'Well, I'll tell you this,' said Nan. 'In my experience, someone coming after you like that means only one thing.'

'What's that?' sighed Vi, waiting for the lecture about how she should stop because it was too dangerous.

'It means you're on the right track,' said Nan. 'Now let's get back to my room. I've got something that might help.'

Back in Autumn Leaves, tea was being served.

'Gerald, leave me a crumpet! You know what you're like!' Nan yelled at a guilty pensioner at the buffet.

'Wendy?' said Nan as they walked back past the

recreation room. 'Any joy?'

'Getting a lot of chatter about that abandoned power station out of town,' said Wendy, whizzing her fingers over the keyboard. 'Something's going down. I'll keep you posted.'

'Excellent. Now, Vi, I'm going to stay here for a few days, give your mum and George some space,' said Nan, walking into her room. 'Besides, they're running a course on knee-replacement ninja skills that I fancy. But before you go, there's something I want you to have. As today has just reminded us, you need to be able to protect yourself. And if your mother won't help you, I will.'

Nan opened a drawer and pulled out a square box wrapped in unicorn paper.

'It was meant for your second birthday, but your mother forbade it,' Nan explained.

Vi ripped off the paper and opened the lid of the box, to reveal a silver watch inside.

'Thanks,' she said, wondering what her two-year-old self would have done with a watch.

'It's an Eye-Spy – your first spy watch,' Nan said proudly, attaching it around Vi's arm. 'No self-respecting spy should be without one.'

Vi looked at the watch on her wrist. It actually

looked pretty cool.

'Now, forgive me – it's been a while since I had this made,' said Nan, putting on her glasses to look at the watch, 'but I think if you press this one . . .'

She pushed the small button on the right of the watch face and a numbered list instantly appeared in thin air. Vi grinned.

'So if you move this outer dial,' her nan said, moving the circle around the watch face slowly between each number, pointing the small red arrow at the top at a different number, 'each hour has a different function. One o'clock is tranquillizer darts, two o'clock is a detonator, three o'clock releases memory-erasing gas, four o'clock amplifies any conversation, five o'clock is a blade and so on and so forth – I can't remember them all, the list will tell you. Do you like it?'

'Best. Present. Ever,' said Vi, fiddling with the watch and making the tiny blade pop out.

'Never leave home without it. You never know when you'll need it,' Nan warned. 'Now, you have to be careful, young lady.'

'Urgh – you sound like Mum,' Vi groaned.

'Good,' said Nan. 'You need to think like her too. It's quite an achievement to be a retired spy, most don't get the chance. I don't always agree with how she does it, but Easter has kept you both safe. Now you need to do the same. Look after yourself. Look after your mother. The Silver Service is here to help.'

She opened her arms and gave Vi the kind of hug that only a nan can.

'You're amazing,' she said. 'Thanks, Nan.'

'You're welcome,' said Indy with a small bow. 'Now, let's go get a crumpet – before Gerald scoffs the lot.'

CHAPTER 11

'No, I don't *think* he's a villain, I'm saying that he *IS* a villain,' Easter blasted down the phone the next day to the fourth divorce lawyer she had called that morning. 'Yes, I know divorce can make it feel that way, but I'm telling you that he is actually a . . . URGH!'

Vi jumped as Easter slammed down the phone. She heard the sound of a rocket blaster in the shed, where the Sprouts were working on Agadoo.

'This is RIDICULOUS!' Easter raged, crossing another name off her list. 'What is the world coming to when you can't just divorce your super-villain ex-husband?'

'Mum, chill,' said Vi. 'Why don't you leave that? I really need to get in early this morning. I—'

'I will *not* chill!' huffed Easter, picking up the phone and dialling the next number on her list. 'There must be someone who can help me.'

'Mum?' Vi tried again. But she knew that once her mum had an idea in her head, there was no stopping her. This was probably useful if you were trying to save the world. Although Vi knew from experience that it was less so if you were trying to convince her not to wear leather trousers on the school run.

'Voicemail!' huffed Easter. 'Why aren't they answering their phone?'

'Because it's eight a.m.?'

'Slackers,' muttered Easter. 'Right – eat up. I'm going on this exercise boot camp today. George will bring you home – he and Russell have got a BlitzBotz practice after school, so you'll have to fit in with their plans, OK?'

'OK,' said Vi, although it wasn't. Today was the day she and Siren were going to visit Frankie the Fence. She already had plans. She needed to talk to Russell.

'Get ready to go,' said Easter. 'Oh, I took your school coat to the dry cleaner. It's hanging in the hall. And here's your lunch – do you want me to put it in your bag?'

'No,' said Vi, quickly grabbing it. She was still hiding the phone there. She didn't want her mum anywhere near her bag.

'And, Vi?' Easter continued, her jaw clenched. 'Until we sort this out I need to ask you . . . no, I need to tell you . . . you cannot see your father.'

'WHAT?' Vi roared. 'You can't do that!'

'Actually, I really can,' Easter insisted with a trembling voice. 'Until I know that I can trust Robert, I cannot leave you with him. Valentine . . . Vi . . . I know this is tough. But it's for the best. I promise you.'

Vi wanted to argue with her mum, to say that it wasn't fair, that she should be allowed to make her own mind up, that Robert had promised he was a good guy now. But one look at her mother's scared, exhausted face silenced her. This was a fight she wasn't going to win.

'Please,' said Easter gently, coming over and stroking Vi's face, 'trust me, baby, OK? I love you. Everything I'm doing is to keep you safe. But you need to keep you safe too. Promise me?'

Vi nodded, ignoring the churning feeling in her guts about her work on the Neurotrol mission. She was trying to get to Rimmington Hall – and save the world from Umbra. Surely her mum would understand that?

She picked up her school coat, refused to acknowledge the 'no, she wouldn't!' screaming inside her head, and headed out to the car.

'Listen,' Vi said to Russell as they crossed the playground on their way to class. 'All you need to do is tell your dad that I'm at a friend's and I'll see you both at home later.'

Russell looked doubtful.

'What friend?' he said. 'You don't . . .'

'I have loads of friends,' said Vi very defensively and slightly inaccurately. 'Just do it, OK?'

'I . . . don't like lying,' he said. 'What if he checks with your mum?'

'She's out tonight so they won't see each other. Besides, I don't know if you've noticed, but they're not exactly chatty at the moment.'

Russell nodded sadly.

'Do you think they'll make up?' he asked.

'I don't know,' said Vi honestly. 'I hope so.'

'Really?' Russell said, wrinkling his nose. 'I thought you'd want them to split up. You haven't seemed that happy to have us around.'

Vi felt a wobble in her stomach. Russell was right. She hadn't been very welcoming to Mr Sprout and Russell. But the thought of not having them at home any more felt . . . weird.

'Why don't we . . . do something?' she said. 'Something to help them get back together?'

'Like what?' said Russell.

'I dunno,' said Vi. 'Ask if we can have a family meal? After BlitzBotz? If we ask, they can't say no. And maybe if they just spend some time together . . .'

'That's a really good idea,' said Russell, giving her a rare smile. 'Thanks.'

'Er . . . you're welcome,' said Vi, not entirely sure what she'd just done as Tom and Sally sidled towards them.

'Here we go,' groaned Russell. 'What do you want?'

'Oh Em Gee – nothing to do with you,' said Sally. 'You're soooo out. We're here to see Vi.'

Vi sighed. What did they want with *her*?

'So, Vi,' said Tom, removing his shades to look

at her with his lovely blue eyes. 'That thing in class yesterday, with Mr Sprout?'

Great, thought Vi. Something else for them to tease her about.

'It was pretty cool,' smiled Tom.

'Er . . . thanks,' said Vi, not sure where to look. She could feel her face turning bright red. She heard Russell gag slightly next to her and gave him a shove in the ribs.

'Yah – everyone's talking about it,' said Sally, pulling out her phone. 'It's soooo in. There's a hashtag and everything.'

Sally showed Vi her social media account, which had a picture of Vi with the hashtag *#ViandMrSproutSmackdown*. Vi smiled. She'd never had a hashtag before. It was kinda cool.

'So what?' said Russell. 'My dad was just tired. Wasn't he, Vi?'

Vi knew she should be defending Mr Sprout. But for once the coolest kids in school weren't teasing her. So she just looked into Tom's eyes. They were so blue . . .

'I hope you're ready for a bruising at BlitzBotz, Sprouty,' Tom grunted. 'I'm going to kick your robot's butt.'

'My robot's really good,' said Russell quietly. 'My dad helped me build it.'

'*Ooooh – my dad helped me build it*,' mimicked Tom unkindly, making Sally fall about laughing. 'Let's hope your dad is better at building robots than he is at getting married. I heard Vi's mum dumped him because she wants to get back together with Vi's real dad.'

'That's not true,' said Russell angrily, looking to Vi to back him up. 'Is it?'

Vi knew she should speak up – that was a horrible thing to say and completely untrue. She got ready to set Tom and Sally straight, but as she opened her mouth, Tom pulled a golden envelope out of his bag.

'It's official – you're soooo in,' said Sally, handing it to her. 'Seeing as you hang with us now, you'd better have one of these.'

Vi opened the envelope. It was an actual invitation. To their actual BlitzBotz party. She looked up at Tom and Sally.

'Welcome to the A-list,' winked Tom, giving her a high five.

'But what about the family meal?' Russell asked. 'After BlitzBotz? You said . . .'

Vi knew that she should turn down Tom and Sally's party and help rebuild her family with Russell.

But she also knew that Tom and Sally were really cool and she really wanted to go to their party.

'Maybe . . . we can do it another time?' she suggested, not meeting Russell's eyes.

'Oh dear,' said Sally, going round behind Russell. 'I think Sprouty's going to cry.'

'I think so too,' said Tom, getting right in Russell's face. 'Are you going to cry, Sprouty?'

Russell looked at Vi, his eyes full of hurt, pleading for her help. She should stand up for him. But the glint of the golden envelope caught her eye. This was her ticket out of being a loser. She couldn't give it up.

'I'm going to class,' Russell muttered.

He picked up his bag and hurried away across the playground.

'Urgh – dramatic exits,' sighed Sally. 'They're soooo out. Come on, Vi. Sit with us in class?'

'Sure,' said Vi, practically running across the playground before they changed their mind. Just as she reached the door, she dropped her golden envelope.

'No!' she gasped as she picked it up from the damp, muddy ground. Her name was on the front, but it was covered in a thick smear of mud.

'Great,' she sighed as she headed for her classroom. She already felt like dirt. And now she had the envelope to prove it.

CHAPTER 12

The second the bell went at 3.15 p.m., Vi was up and out of class. Even though Easter never let her, Year Sixes were allowed to walk home on their own, so no one challenged Vi rushing out of the school gates and jumping on the bus that took her the short ride to the pier. As she alighted, it wasn't hard to spot Siren – she was the only person wearing a satin green cocktail dress at 3.31 in the afternoon.

'Hey kiddo,' she smiled. 'Good to see you. I was worried I was going to be late. I had to treat my athlete's foot. My shoes are like the inside of a snow globe.'

'OK . . .' said Vi as they headed down Norton-on-Sea Pier to the ageing amusement arcade at its end. Vi shuddered. Danny's Dreamland looked like the crime scene from every *Scooby Doo* cartoon ever. At the entrance was a plastic clown that let out a creepy laugh when someone walked past. Although, having met Auguste, it was now the second creepiest clown Vi knew. 'So, tell me about Frankie.'

'Frankie the Fence,' Siren began. 'If you want to know where any stolen goods have gone – or if you need some stolen yourself – Frankie is your man. He is the Robin Hood of the criminal underworld. If Robin Hood had kept all his money to himself and stolen from the poor, the rich and his own mother. With your dad retired, Frankie would have been Umbra's thief of choice. And Frankie might be a two-bit robber, but he's loyal. Getting him to talk won't be easy.'

'So what's the plan?' Vi asked.

'Frankie has two weaknesses,' Siren explained. 'The first one is quizzing.'

'Quizzing?' asked Vi. 'As in . . . doing quizzes?'

'The very same,' breathed Siren, picking something out of her teeth. 'He's obsessed. I'm no psychologist, but I think it's a desperate need to earn something legitimately after a life of crime. That, or something to do with his mother.'

'He had a difficult childhood?' Vi asked.

'No idea,' sighed Siren. 'Dawn just really likes quizzes.'

'What's his other weakness?' Vi asked.

'He's a terrible liar,' Siren replied. 'The man always picks his nose when he's telling a whopper.'

'Now that's a tell,' smirked Vi.

'Follow me,' said Siren, heading into the arcade.

'HAHAHAHAHAHAHAHA!' screeched the creepy clown, making Vi jump out of her skin.

'Now, kiddo,' said Siren. 'I'm not gonna lie. Sometimes to extract information, you have to use . . . dubious methods. You might see things you don't want to. If you'd prefer to stay out here, that's fine.'

Vi smiled. Siren couldn't have made it sound more appealing if she'd tried.

'I'm fine,' she said. 'Let's do this.'

They walked through the arcade, past the clanking and whirring of the aged machines. A gaggle of teenagers were hopefully pumping two-pence pieces into a machine that had hundreds of them tantalizingly teetering on the edge of a drop. Vi looked at the prizes they were hoping to win. A small pencil and a car keyring. For the money they'd spent on that machine, they probably could have bought a pack of pencils and an actual car.

She still really wanted a go, though.

Siren slunk on, past machines that required you to shoot, drive or blast your way through their game. The collective noise was overwhelming and the fake light added to the sense of otherworldliness. It was a horrible place. Vi couldn't wait to be out of there.

'There he is,' said Siren, pulling up and pointing to a spindly, needle-nosed white man in front of the MegaBrain machine. He was dressed all in check, from his suit to his hat, with his trousers not quite meeting his socks. The pencil moustache over his thin lips wavered as he chewed what looked like a small stick, jabbing quiz buttons with contempt.

Siren looked around the dingy arcade.

'Your environment can be your best weapon,' she whispered. 'Make sure you use it. Follow me.'

'Who was the second man on the moon? ARE YOU 'AVING A LARF?' Frankie shouted at the machine. 'Me dog could answer that and 'ee's bin dead since 2004 . . . It's Buzz Aldrin, you plum!

Gimme strengff!'

Siren sidled up behind him and tapped him on the shoulder.

'Hey Frankie,' she pouted. 'Wanna play?'

'S-S-S-Siren,' Frankie stammered, spinning around and patting his oily black hair. 'It's really you. I'm your biggest fan.'

'I know,' Siren said, shimmying over as Dave popped out from behind a pinball machine and started playing saxophone behind her. 'I got your letters. They were . . . quite something.'

'I never sent you no letters,' said Frankie, his finger creeping towards his left nostril.

'Whatever you say,' said Siren, winking at Vi. 'So I need to ask you some— Dave!'

Dave stopped playing and looked over.

'Go and play Pac-Man,' Siren instructed. 'We need to talk.'

Dave saluted coolly, picked up the fifty pence someone had thrown into his sax case and headed across the arcade.

'As I was saying,' smiled Siren, 'it's not often someone sends me letters like yours. It's so good to meet a fellow cruciverbalist. We could have a lot of fun together.'

'Am I old enough to know what that means?' Vi whispered.

'Cruciverbalist,' Frankie repeated. 'Noun. A person who enjoys or is skilled at solving crosswords. Siren is a general knowledge legend – she was Mastermind twenty-five times. It would have been twenty-six, but she nicked the trophy before the final and was disqualified.'

'Correct,' smiled Siren, as Frankie wiped a bead of sweat from his forehead. 'I've got an idea. Why don't we have a quiz? Right here. Right now.'

'YOU ARE YANKIN' MY CHAIN!' Frankie exploded. 'That would be . . . it would be . . . YES!'

'OK, then,' said Siren, sitting backwards on a chair. 'Here's how we play.'

Frankie grabbed a chair, nodding like an eager puppy.

'Yeah?' he panted.

'My friend Valentine has some questions for you,' Siren explained.

'I need to find the Neurotrol,' Vi added.

'Neuro . . . what? Never . . . never 'eard of it,' stammered Frankie, filling his right nostril with finger. 'You got the wrong geeza.'

'Then you have nothing to hide,' smouldered

Siren. 'You ask me a general knowledge question. If I get it right, you have to answer one of Valentine's questions. Deal?'

Vi watched Frankie squirm in his chair. This was a conflicted man.

'Or I could just leave,' Siren added, pushing herself forward to stand up. 'I really need to see my chiropodist. My left foot looks like the runner-up in an ugly potato competition.'

'No!' cried Frankie. 'Please stay. I'll . . . I'll play.'

He took a steadying breath as Siren emitted a small fart.

'Pardon, Mrs Arden,' breathed Siren as Vi moved discreetly away. 'There's a rabbit in my garden.'

'All right, Q-question One,' Frankie stuttered, mopping his brow with a dirty hankie. 'What is the common name of *Amanita phalloides*, the most poisonous British mushroom?'

'The Death Cap,' Siren replied without hesitation. 'Responsible for ninety per cent of fungus-related fatalities. Speaking of fungal growths, I must get my toenails seen to . . .'

'Is she right?' Vi asked Frankie.

'Correct,' shuddered Frankie, breathing hard.

'Vi?' Siren asked.

'Did you steal the Neurotrol?' Vi asked.

'I don't steal, I . . . relocate,' he said, rummaging in his nose.

Vi smiled to herself. Just like her putpocketing.

'Well, if you won't play fair and answer Vi's questions,' pouted Siren, standing up, 'I won't play and answer yours.'

'All right!' Frankie cried. 'All right! Yes, yes, I did! Nicked it out of some old science lab last week.'

Vi felt a thrill surge through her body. She was on to something.

'Where is it?' she gabbled. 'Where is it now?'

'Nah – fair play, darlin', a question for a question,' said Frankie.

'Go ahead,' challenged Siren.

'Question Two,' stuttered Frankie. 'How many nanometres are there in a millimetre?' Vi did a quick calculation in her head. She made it ten thousand.

'One million,' said Siren confidently.

Vi shrugged. Close enough.

'Correct,' said Frankie uneasily.

'Where is the Neurotrol?' Vi asked over her

pounding heart. 'Where have you hidden it?'

'I haven't!' said Frankie desperately. 'I just steal . . . relocate . . . the gear to order – none of my business what happens to it. I just took the money and delivered the Neurotrol to my client.'

Vi and Siren both stared at Frankie. No nose-picking. He was telling the truth.

'Who's your client?' Vi asked. 'Umbra?'

'I . . . I can't tell you that,' said Frankie. 'They'll destroy me.'

'Oh, that's a shame,' said Siren, standing to leave. 'Then there's no point in us carrying on.'

'Wait!' panted Frankie, a new sheen of sweat breaking out on his brow. 'I'll talk. But first, what is the capital of . . . Zambia?'

'Rats,' Siren whispered. 'I'm terrible with capital cities.'

Vi racked her brain. She knew this. What was it?

'I'm going to have to hurry you,' grinned Frankie. 'That's five . . . four . . . three . . . two . . .'

'LUSAKA!' Vi screamed out, Mr Sprout's voice suddenly amplifying in her brain. 'It's Lusaka!'

Wow. It turned out that some of his useless knowledge was actually useful. Who knew?

Frankie sulked in his chair.

'Well, is it?' asked Siren. 'Frankie?'

'Correct,' grumbled Frankie. 'Bums.'

'So?' asked Vi, her nerves tingling with excitement. 'Who was it? Who did you give the Neurotrol to? It was Umbra, wasn't it?'

Frankie let out a long slow breath.

'It weren't Umbra,' he whispered. 'Well, not exactly . . . It was . . . it was . . . it was Sir Charge.'

Vi's heart thundered in her chest.

No. It couldn't have been.

'Robert?' Siren gasped.

'My dad?' Vi exclaimed.

'VI?'

Robert's voice boomed across the arcade.

'What on earth are you doing here? Explain yourself.'

Vi turned around in a rage.

'No – you explain yourself!' she exploded. 'You swore you weren't working for Umbra! You said you were good now! So why do you have the Neurotrol?'

Robert's face drained of colour.

'Shhhh! Vi – I can explain everything, I promise,' said Robert, looking around nervously as he walked over to her. 'This isn't what you think. But you cannot be wandering around on your own, it's too dangerous.'

'You sound just like Mum,' Vi snapped, shaking his hand off her shoulder. 'Hang on – how did you even know I was here?'

Robert sighed.

'Your backpack,' he said. 'I put a tracking device in it yesterday.'

'WHAT?' Vi exploded. 'That's such an invasion of privacy!'

'I'm just trying to keep you safe,' he said. 'Speaking of which, you need to give me that phone and we need to get you home before your mother—'

'VALENTINE DAY!'

Vi's heart turned to ice as her mother's voice sliced through the arcade.

'Easter Day!' Frankie cried. 'I haven't seen you since I relocated that—'

A deathly stare from Vi's mother stopped Frankie the Fence dead.

'Well, er . . . nice to see you all,' said Frankie, scampering off out of the arcade as fast as his spindly legs could carry him.

'Mum?' Vi exclaimed. 'How did you know?'

'I *knew* you were up to something,' said Easter, charging towards her. 'That's why I put a tracking device in your school coat.'

'What is wrong with you both?' Valentine shouted. 'You lied to me!'

Easter turned and fixed her with a stare that Vi suspected was the last thing many people had seen.

'Do you want to argue about telling the truth right now?'

Vi said nothing. No. No, she really didn't.

'And as for you,' said Easter, turning to Siren.

'What about me, sister?' said Siren. 'Don't take another step. Seriously, I have BO that could wake the dead.'

'Siren – stand down,' said Robert. 'Easter, I had no idea . . .'

'Of course you didn't!' raged Easter. 'That's just your problem, Robert, you have no idea how to be a parent. This is why I banned her from seeing you . . .'

'You did *what*?' Robert roared. 'What gives you the right—'

'TEN YEARS OF RAISING HER BY

MYSELF GIVES ME THE RIGHT!' Easter screamed. 'You've been back five minutes and already you have my daughter in some den of iniquity with a snotty thief and some . . . hussy with a hygiene problem.'

'Watch it, lady,' said Siren. 'I have aim like an arrow and breath like a litter tray. You don't want to be on the wrong end of either.'

But Easter didn't care about Siren. She only had eyes for Robert. Eyes full of anger.

'I warned you, Robert,' she hissed. 'I told you that if you dragged my daughter into your seedy world, you aren't fit to be her father. I've found a lawyer. We're going to court. And when I'm done, you will NEVER see Valentine again.'

'NO!' shouted Vi, hot, confused tears coming to her eyes. 'Please, Mum, I just need to talk to him, I need to understand something. I'm the problem here . . .'

'You've never been the problem, Vi,' Easter said. 'But I have the solution. Come on. I'm taking you home.'

'Robert?' Vi cried imploringly.

Robert just stood with his head hanging down.

'Go with your mother,' he said. 'We'll sort

everything out. I promise.'

Vi didn't believe him. But as her mother hurried her out of the arcade, past the creepy clown into the piercing afternoon light, she realized that right now, she really didn't have any choice.

CHAPTER 13

'You lied to me, Vi,' said Easter unevenly as they walked into the house after a silent journey home. Her face was a mixture of disappointment and sadness. This was so much worse than the shouting.

'I didn't mean to, I just wanted to—'

'Is there anything else I need to know?' Easter said, staring at Vi intensely. 'Because you should tell me – now. Are you hiding anything else?'

Vi thought about all the things she was hiding from her mother. It was time for a confession.

'Mum,' she began, after a deep breath. 'I . . . I . . . got chocolate all over the armchair in the kitchen. I turned the cushion over so you wouldn't see it. I'm really sorry.'

There. Confession made.

Her mum looked at her for a moment. She seemed . . . relieved.

'Is that all?' she sighed. 'I don't care about the furniture. I care about you. Promise me, Vi. Promise me there's nothing else you're keeping from me.'

'No,' said Vi, her heart hammering in her chest. She was so close to cracking this mission. If she told Mum now, she'd never stop Umbra and get to Rimmington Hall. 'That's everything.'

'Good,' said Easter, finally taking a breath. 'I know this is hard, Vi. But you have to trust me. Go upstairs and do your homework. George and Russell will be back from BlitzBotz practice soon and I said I'd help at the PTA disco tonight. We'll talk tomorrow.'

'OK,' said Vi, trudging up the stairs. She felt awful. But now she knew where the Neurotrol was, if she could just get it from Robert . . .

'And, Vi,' said her mum, making Vi's heart quicken again. She turned around to see Easter smiling at the bottom of the stairs. 'I love you.'

'I love you too, Mum.'

They exchanged a warm smile. It was all going to be OK.

‘Hey,’ said Easter, picking up Vi’s backpack. ‘Don’t forget your bag.’

‘Er, Mum . . . I’ll get it,’ said Vi, heading down to fetch the broken bag herself. But it was too late. Easter had already tossed the backpack up the stairs, making the broken zip fly open in mid-air and the contents explode everywhere. Everything in Vi’s bag trickled down the stairs like a waterfall – her books, her pencil case, the thirty empty sweet wrappers she’d hidden in there. And then, right at the bottom, landing exactly by Easter’s left foot, her mobile phone.

Easter picked it up incredulously.

‘Where did you get this? Was it your father?’

‘No . . . Yes . . . Well, sort of,’ said Vi. ‘It’s complicated.’

‘I might have guessed,’ said Easter, her eyes full of hurt disappointment again. ‘You know how I feel about these. Do you care about anything I say any more?’

‘Mum . . .’ Vi began, unable to look at her mother’s betrayed face. ‘I – I’m sorry.’

‘So am I,’ said Easter, dropping Vi’s phone into her handbag. ‘We’ll talk tomorrow.’

Vi tried to think of something to say. But she

had nothing. She admitted defeat and trudged upstairs.

But halfway up, a familiar voice caught her ear.

'Easter, I mean, Susan. Are you OK?'

It was Honey B. She was in the kitchen. Why?

'Robert,' glowered Easter. 'He's just a . . . what are you doing here?'

'Are we secure?' Honey asked.

'Not again,' Easter huffed. 'What is it this time?'

Honey opened the living-room door, revealing a new and unfamiliar hat stand. Vi looked again. The hat stand was actually painted on a camouflage coat. And it wasn't a hat stand at all. It was The Cardinal.

'All clear?' he whispered into the kitchen.

'All clear,' sighed Easter as The Wolf clambered out from inside the sofa. 'What do you want?'

The Cardinal walked into the kitchen and closed the door behind him. Vi cursed under her breath. Agadoo wasn't there – Mr Sprout and Russell were at the BlitzBotz practice. How was she going to . . .

She looked down at the Eye-Spy watch Nan had given her. Wasn't there a . . .

She turned the dial to four o'clock.

Voice amplification activated, the watch flashed. Suddenly she could hear everything.

'That's just absurd!' she heard Easter say. 'Valentine is an eleven-year-old girl! There's no way she's mixed up in this!'

'We have received intelligence that she is in possession of the Neurotrol,' The Cardinal said. 'It is imperative we extract it from her.'

Vi felt a tsunami of butterflies in her stomach. Why did SPIDER think she had the Neurotrol?

'We had reports of an incident involving a firearm at Autumn Leaves yesterday,' The Cardinal continued.

'It was probably the quiz night, you know what they're like,' Easter replied.

'Nevertheless, one of our operatives reported seeing Valentine there,' The Cardinal insisted. 'We need to speak to her.'

'Great,' muttered Vi to herself. She'd known someone was following her yesterday. But who?

'Valentine!' came Easter's irritable voice from the kitchen door. 'Can you come here, please, baby?'

Vi walked down the stairs and into the kitchen. She could feel all eyes on her. It didn't feel good.

'Agent Lynx, please give us a moment,' The Cardinal ordered, rather than asked. 'SPIDER protocol dictates that we interview suspects privately.'

'Over my dead body!' Easter snarled, grabbing Vi to her. It was the first time Vi had felt safe all day. 'She's a child. And she's not a suspect, she's my daughter!'

'Easter . . . Susan,' Honey whispered gently, taking Mum's hand. 'The quickest way for all this to go away is to let them ask their questions. I'm her godmother – you made me legal guardian, in case anything ever . . . I'll make sure she's OK.'

Easter looked at Vi, her eyes full of protective concern.

'Vi?' she asked gently. 'Is this all right with you?'

Vi wanted to scream that, no, it wasn't, that she was scared and she wanted her mum. But she also wanted to be a spy. She would have to face interrogations. This was good training.

'It's fine,' she smiled. 'You go.'

'I'll be right outside,' Easter grumbled. 'You have five minutes.'

She walked out of the kitchen and shut the door.

‘Now, Valentine,’ said Honey B, pulling up a chair. ‘We just need to ask you a few questions. You’re not in any trouble.’

‘Not yet,’ said The Cardinal sternly. Vi looked him square in the eyes. She needed to tough this one out.

‘Has anyone . . . given you anything lately?’ Honey asked. ‘Maybe asked you to look after it? Hide it for them?’

‘No,’ said Vi honestly. She’d putpocketed some stuff, but that wasn’t the same thing.

‘You see,’ Honey cajoled, ‘something’s gone missing. Something very important. And we have reason to believe that you have it.’

‘What is it?’ said Vi, forcing her eyes wide open to look as innocent as possible. It wasn’t easy. ‘Have you lost your keys? Mum’s always doing that.’

‘No,’ said Honey, laughing insincerely. ‘Nothing like that. We’re looking for a microchip. We suspect it’s been hidden inside something – a transmitter. Maybe a walkie-talkie? A remote control? A mobile phone?’

Vi tried not to gasp as the realization hit her like a missile.

Oh . . . that's . . . just an old phone, Robert had stammered.

Her phone.

I keep meaning to get it . . . recycled . . .

The phone she had putpocketed from her dad's car.

It . . . it doesn't belong to me. And the owner wants it . . .

Her phone *was* the Neurotrol.

So that's why Mr Sprout had acted so weirdly in class – he was being controlled by the Neurotrol. That's why Robert had wanted the phone back. That's why Umbra had tried to steal her backpack. And that's what SPIDER was looking for now.

She had it! She had the Neurotrol! If she took it straight to Rimmington Hall, she'd have accomplished her mission. She could be a spy!

But first she had to say something to Honey B.

Vi looked her godmother straight in the eye.

'No,' she said calmly. 'I haven't got anything.'

'ENOUGH!' roared The Cardinal, slamming his hand on the table. 'WHERE IS IT? WHERE IS THE NEUROTROL? DO YOU HAVE ANY IDEA HOW SERIOUS THIS IS?'

The kitchen door was kicked open and Easter flew into the room. Between two seconds, The Cardinal was in a judo hold on the floor.

'DON'T YOU DARE SHOUT AT MY DAUGHTER!' she shouted. 'THAT'S MY JOB!'

Vi tried not to smile. Her mum was so awesome.

'Agent Lynx!' The Cardinal gasped. 'Agent Lynx! Unhand me at once!'

'Easter!' Honey B exclaimed, pulling her best friend off her boss.

Vi couldn't resist a smirk. She looked up at The Wolf, who was staring straight at her. He didn't believe her one bit.

'That's enough!' cried The Cardinal, breaking free from Easter's grip with a lot of help from Honey. 'We have a warrant to search Valentine's possessions. Resist and I'll have you arrested.'

'You . . . you can't do that,' said Easter, as The Cardinal slapped a piece of paper in her hand. 'I'm going to—'

'Easter,' Honey warned as The Cardinal and The Wolf stormed upstairs to Vi's room. 'Step aside. If you're going to court with Robert, how's it going to look if you've been arrested? Let them do their job. Vi's got nothing to hide. Have you, Vi?'

Vi summoned some tears to her eyes. She was better at innocent than she thought.

'No,' she sniffed. 'I haven't done anything wrong.'

'Come here, baby,' said Easter, pulling her into her strong embrace. 'This will all be over in a minute. They're not going to find anything. And if you think you're going up there alone, you've got another think coming.'

Vi tried not to smile as Easter leapt up the stairs. She knew that SPIDER wasn't going to find the phone. It was in her mum's handbag. For the first time ever, she was grateful for Mum's paranoia.

She waited in the kitchen, the dull thuds of her room being searched the only noise in the house. Even though Vi knew they wouldn't find anything, her heart wouldn't steady. What if they looked in Mum's handbag? What if they forced her to talk? What if they arrested her and sent her to prison?

After what seemed like hours, the SPIDER agents reappeared downstairs. The Cardinal glared at Vi.

'We have places we put people who work

against us,' he said darkly. 'So if we discover you lied to us . . .'

Vi breathed half a sigh of relief. They hadn't found anything. She was OK. For now.

'Get out of my house!' Easter snapped, pointing to the door. The Cardinal stormed straight out. The Wolf gave Vi a long, significant look, then turned to leave.

Vi watched as the SPIDER agents left the house, Honey giving Mum a reassuring squeeze on her way past. The moment the door shut, Easter gathered Vi into her arms.

'Are you OK?' she asked, patting all over Vi's body for some imagined hurt.

'I'm fine, Mum – chill,' said Vi with a smile.

'That's it, I'm cancelling tonight,' said Easter. 'There's no way I'm going out, you need me here.'

'Mum, I'm fine!' said Vi, not relishing the thought of a night with her mum watching her every move. 'You go – you could do with a night out. Everything's fine, really.'

The sound of keys in the door announced that the Sprouts were home. Vi looked over at her mum's bag. She needed to get the Neurotrol back before Mum realized she had it. If she got Nan to take her and the Neurotrol to Rimmington Hall, they'd surely have to let her in . . .

'Sorry we're a bit late,' said Mr Sprout, stopping short in the hallway. 'I hope I haven't held you up?'

'Don't worry about it,' Easter replied distractedly. 'I promised I'd help with the stupid PTA seventies disco tonight. But I don't know if . . .'

'Mum, I told you, I'm fine,' said Vi, trying not to look at the handbag. 'You go. Have a good time.'

'I see,' said Mr Sprout. 'They've let you back after that business at the casino night with the Tilsleys?'

Vi looked at the handbag again and started to sidle towards it. If she could just reach her left hand down . . .

'I might be late,' said Easter, snatching up the bag and putting it on her shoulder. 'Is that OK?'

'Sure,' said George. 'I'll sleep in the spare room. If that's all right . . .'

'Of course it is,' said Easter. 'George . . . this is your home. I miss you so much.'

Easter leant in for a kiss with Mr Sprout. Vi

could see the phone poking out of her bag. Perhaps she could . . .

But Mr Sprout ducked out of the way, making Mum swerve out of Vi's reach.

'Fine,' sighed Easter, as Vi silently cursed. 'Please can you give Vi dinner? And she's not to be too late to bed, she has . . .'

'A school trip tomorrow,' said George. 'I know.'

'Of course you do,' said Easter sadly. 'I'll see you in the morning.'

Easter moped out of the house, taking the Neurotrol with her. Vi silently punched the wall. She needed to get to the disco and retrieve the Neurotrol before her mum could activate it. If Easter switched it on, even accidentally, any adult exposed to it for more than a few minutes would have more than the dodgy PTA buffet to worry about – their brains would explode. Vi couldn't take that risk. But how was she going to get away?

She ran into the kitchen, and was distracted by Russell laying out his homework at the kitchen table. She noticed the muddy marks on his books. It looked like he'd had another encounter with Tom.

'Hey,' she said sheepishly. Russell looked at her

but said nothing. The whole guilty horror of how she had abandoned him earlier came flooding back. 'Listen, I know you're not my greatest fan right now, but I need you to cover for me while I . . .'

'I found this in the hall – is it yours?' Mr Sprout asked her, waving the golden envelope as he went to reheat some leftovers. It felt really comforting having him back in the kitchen.

'Yeah,' she said vaguely. 'Can I go?'

Mr Sprout read the invitation. Mum would never let her. But if she got *his* permission, surely that counted . . .

'I'm afraid you need to ask your mother,' Mr Sprout said gently. 'And anyway . . .'

'What?' Vi asked quickly. She had to get to the school. And she had to go to that party.

'It's on Saturday,' Mr Sprout said. 'After BlitzBotz. Are you invited too, Russell? I hoped we might be celebrating afterwards.'

Russell looked up. His silence said it all. Vi felt the knife turn a little more in her heart.

'It's fine,' said Russell quietly, finishing his homework in record time. 'Let Vi go to her party. It's no big deal.'

'No big deal? Are you sure?' Mr Sprout laughed. 'You've been looking forward to it for months, we've worked so hard on Agadoo . . .'

'I'm sure,' said Russell, getting down from the table and trudging towards his room. 'Let Vi do what she wants. Don't worry about dinner for me, Dad. I'm not hungry.'

He walked out of the room and Vi heard his heavy footsteps on the stairs. Mr Sprout watched him go, before turning back to Vi and putting Mum's latest fusion dish – spiced snapper cullen skink – in front of her. She started to gobble it down. If she hurried, she could make it to school before the disco started.

'Valentine?' he asked in that sing-song tone adults use when they're trying to disguise something really important. 'Is Russell OK? At school, I mean?'

Vi stuffed a spoonful of soup between her jaws, partly for speed, partly so she didn't have to answer. How could she tell Russell's dad that, no, Russell wasn't OK? He was being picked on by the cool kids. Which now, she realized with mixed feelings, included her.

'You'd have to ask him,' she said, swallowing

quickly. 'We don't really talk much at school.'

'I see,' said Mr Sprout. He looked really worried. 'Do me a favour – would you keep an eye on him? I'm not asking you to spy or anything . . .'

Mr Sprout stopped and laughed at his own joke. Vi remembered to laugh as well, as though the very idea of anyone spying in their household was utterly absurd.

'. . . but could you just look out for him? Let me know if anyone's being unkind or giving him a hard time?'

Vi started coughing violently. Some snapper had got caught in her throat.

'Oh no – here,' said Mr Sprout, patting her hard on her back before giving her a glass of water. 'Did you know that about three thousand droplets of saliva are expelled in a single cough and some of them fly out at speeds of up to fifty miles per hour?'

'I didn't,' gasped Vi as she drank the water. She'd missed Mr Sprout's geeky facts. In fact, she'd kinda missed Mr Sprout's geeky everything.

The coughing subsided.

'Thanks,' she smiled.

'No worries,' said Mr Sprout. At least nearly choking had changed the conversation.

'Er, I'm going to go up too,' said Vi. 'Long day – I could do with an early night.'

'Wow,' said Mr Sprout looking at her half-eaten dinner. 'Something I said?'

'No,' Vi said quickly, not wanting to hurt his feelings. 'It's . . . it's really good to hang out with you. At home, I mean.'

'Thanks,' said Mr Sprout, looking genuinely happy. 'That . . . that means a lot.'

'You're welcome,' said Vi, feeling herself blush a bit. 'See you in the morning.'

'See you,' said Mr Sprout. 'And, Vi?'

'Yes?' she said, trying not to sound too impatient.

'Try not to worry about me and your mum,' Mr Sprout said shyly. 'I . . . I do love her very much.'

'Good,' said Vi, meaning it. 'She loves you too.'

'Thanks,' said Mr Sprout, looking even happier. 'And we've got an exciting day at Dulworth Cove tomorrow. Did you know that the depth of water there changes ten metres with the tides? It'll be fascinating.'

‘Can’t wait,’ said Vi, sprinting upstairs and pounding on Russell’s door as hard as she could without alerting Mr Sprout.

‘Russell?’ she asked. ‘Russell, please, I need to talk to you.’

There was a pause before the door opened.

‘OK,’ she began, ‘I need to ask you about—’

‘Oh – so you *do* know who I am?’ said Russell darkly.

‘Look, I’m sorry about earlier,’ Vi said. ‘It’s just that Tom and Sally—’

‘Are more important than me,’ said Russell.

‘Yes,’ said Vi instinctively. ‘I mean – no!’

‘It doesn’t matter,’ sighed Russell. ‘What do you want?’

Vi didn’t have time to make up a lie, so she told Russell the whole story of Umbra, the Neurotrol and the danger it now posed to a roomful of parents.

‘So if your dad asks where I am, I’m asleep,’ said Vi. ‘I have to get to the school.’

‘Wow,’ said Russell. ‘That Neurotrol is scary stuff. Although the tech sounds awesome, I wonder what frequency it—’

‘Russell!’ said Vi before he geeked out. ‘Will

you help me?'

Russell stopped and looked at her. He seemed almost . . . pleased.

'Yes,' he said as she checked the landing to make sure Mr Sprout was still in the kitchen. 'I've got some stuff that might come in handy.'

'Thanks,' she said as he disappeared back into his room, 'but you'll have to tell me how to use it.'

'No need,' said Russell, reappearing with his trusty anorak and a rucksack. 'I'm coming too.'

CHAPTER 14

The school hall was decked out with streamers, a flashing dance floor and a giant disco ball shedding glimmering diamonds all over the room.

'Are you sure your dad isn't going to notice we've gone?' Vi asked, worried about Mr Sprout raising the alarm.

'Nah,' said Russell casually. 'The new series of *Discoveries That Changed Science* just dropped. We've got about three days before he realizes we're missing.'

'Good to know,' said Vi, as she watched the parents milling around, drinking and chatting in their seventies disco outfits. There were two disasters Vi needed to prevent: one, a room full of exploding parents; two, a room full of middle-aged people dancing in spandex. Both were potentially tragic.

'There she is,' said Russell, pointing across the room to where Easter was running the bar and chatting with a tall black woman wearing a flared white satin catsuit, red shades and a huge seventies Afro wig. Vi barely recognized her – that was Tyler Carter's mum, chair of the PTA.

'OK – you said that the Neurotrol was switched off?'

'Yes,' said Vi confidently. She hadn't dared switch it on since yesterday, in the classroom, in case she got caught with it.

'Good – so if we just go to your mum and explain what she has—'

'No way!' said Vi, holding Russell back. 'I just lied to SPIDER! I lied to her! If she finds out I'm involved with the Neurotrol now, she is going to go ballistic.'

'Better than her exploding,' Russell pointed out.

'I know that,' said Vi. 'But if she finds out I've been working on a dangerous spy mission, she will ban me from life.'

'Vi – this is getting serious,' said Russell. 'SPIDER is involved. Umbra is involved. You could be in big trouble. You need your mum's help.'

'No,' said Vi stubbornly. She wasn't going to fail her mission. Not when she was so close. 'All we need to do is get the Neurotrol back. Then I can take it to Rimmington Hall and prove I can be a spy. How would you feel if someone said you couldn't go to the Tech Academy?'

Russell pushed his glasses up his nose.

'Really rubbish,' he admitted.

'Then help me out. Follow me.'

The two of them crawled past the window towards the slightly open fire door. Vi checked to see if anyone was standing nearby – the coast was clear, so they slipped inside and hid beneath one of the tables, their presence concealed by a tablecloth.

'Our best bet,' said Russell, 'is to close this thing down. If I can get to the fuse box, I can cut the power – then everyone will have to go home. Less risk to the parents, easier for you to get the phone back at home.'

'OK,' said Vi. 'You do that. I'll try to get the Neurotrol, make sure she can't switch it on. I'll meet you back here.'

'Good luck,' said Russell as he crawled out of the gym.

Vi looked at her Eye-Spy watch to see what might help her. Tranquillizing her mum seemed a bit extreme – and in any case, that would draw too much attention. She could see her mum's bag on the floor. She just needed to get to it . . .

As she was about to make her move, Vi heard two voices in platform shoes standing by her table.

'I'm telling you, darling, they are delicious,' said a man's voice. 'Best ever.'

'Well, you make sure that everyone sees you eating them,' said a woman's voice in an irritated whisper. 'No one has touched my sausage rolls for the past three PTA events. I'm a laughing stock.'

Vi recognized the man's voice. He was Arthur Tilsley's dad. The one Easter had arrested at the casino night.

'Well, it's their loss, dear,' the man said through a mouthful. 'They're utterly divine.'

'Good,' said Mrs Tilsley. 'I'm going to get us a drink.'

'Make mine a double,' muttered Mr Tilsley, sounding like he was spitting something out. A soggy napkin landed just in front of Vi, filled with half-chewed sausage roll.

Vi gagged and carried on, making her way through the tables, crawling under tablecloths.

'OK, you crazy cats!' the DJ cheesed. 'Get ready because in just a few minutes, we are going to get our groove thang awwwwwwwwwwnnnnn!'

Vi shuddered. The thought of all these parents getting their groove thing anywhere was even less appetizing than Mrs Tilsley's sausage rolls. She crawled around until she reached Tyler's mum and Easter.

'No, Mindy – I think you're doing a fantastic job as chair,' she heard her mum say.

'Thanks, Susan,' said Mindy. 'I just worry that people think I'm too bossy, that I'm trying to pressure people into these events . . .'

'Not at all!' Easter insisted. Vi bet she was blinking. 'Everyone is super-grateful. Now, when are we getting started? I could do with a good dance – I need to shake my stress off.'

Vi stretched her fingers out. The bag was just out of reach, but if she stretched just a little bit more . . .

'I hope everyone has a good time,' Mindy

chipped in, knocking the bag out of reach with her foot. 'I'm not sure about the buffet, perhaps asking everyone to bring something was a bit cheap.'

'You worry too much,' said Easter. 'And if you think you've got problems – let me tell you about my ex . . .'

Vi stretched towards the bag. She was getting close, closer, nearly close enough.

'Oh, I feel your pain,' said Mindy, shifting her feet and kicking the bag further away. 'I have so many problems with Tyler's dad. Different girlfriend every week, doesn't show up to collect Tyler, when he does he just feeds him rubbish and gives him all the things I say he can't have. It's only by checking Tyler's phone that I know half the things they're up to.'

'You . . . you check your child's phone?' Easter asked as Vi's fingers finally made contact with the bag. She slipped her hand inside. Now where was the phone?

'Don't you?' said Mindy, kicking the bag and Vi's hand. Vi froze. Had she noticed her? 'I wouldn't let Tyler use a knife unsupervised, it's too dangerous. Why wouldn't I do the same with a mobile phone?'

'Good point,' Easter agreed, suddenly snatching up her bag and yanking Vi's hand. Vi silently yelled and held her wrist under the table. Brilliant. *Thanks, Mindy.* Vi peeked out to see Easter rummaging around in her bag and pulling out the Neurotrol. 'I think I'll take your advice. No time like the present.'

'It's the safest way,' said Mindy the big idiot. Vi wondered if she even had a brain to explode.

Vi watched her mum turn the Neurotrol around in her hands. For a spy, she was really bad with technology, maybe she wouldn't . . .

Click!

Easter turned the phone on. The Neurotrol was activated.

'And now,' the DJ announced over the mic, 'it's time for my seventies megamix, from the time when . . . *Everybody was Kung Fu Fighting*!'

'Come on!' Mindy squealed. 'Let's dance!'

Immediately Easter obeyed, dropping her handbag on the floor. She'd never normally do that – she was almost as protective of her handbag as she was of Vi. Vi felt a cold panic rise in her chest. The Neurotrol must be controlling her mum.

The handbag landed next to Vi as she heard Easter's determined strides pace across the dance floor. Vi grabbed it and rummaged through it.

No Neurotrol.

She watched Easter head to the dance floor with a Neurotrol-shaped bulge in her back pocket.

'I couldn't do it,' said Russell, suddenly appearing under the table next to her. 'The fuse box is inside the caretaker's office.'

'What's the problem?' asked Vi.

'The caretaker,' said Russell. 'He's sitting in there watching a show about bathroom grouting. I'll never get past him. How are you getting on?'

'Disaster,' said Vi, starting back around the tables towards her mum. 'Mum's switched on the Neurotrol. It's in her back pocket.'

'What do we do?' asked Russell, crawling behind her.

'I don't know,' said Vi as they arrived at the buffet again. 'But we've only got a few minutes to do it, or this place will be filled with exploding brains.'

The dance floor lit up as the adults gathered together. But as the song reached its chorus, they stopped dancing . . . and started doing martial arts moves. Mr Tilsley – who Vi could now see was wearing rainbow-coloured flares and a matching bandana around the long, brown wig that covered his usually white, bald head – nearly split his trousers attempting a karate kick, until Easter showed him how to do it properly by smacking the buffet table with one.

'Oh no – they'll do whatever the song tells them to,' Vi realized as the parents started fighting each other. 'And how are cats fast as lightning?'

'Er, hang on,' asked Russell. 'Why aren't we doing this?'

'The Neurotrol only works on adult brain-waves,' Vi recalled from SPIDER's visit. 'I guess kids' brains are just wired differently.'

'Thankfully,' shuddered Russell.

'For sure,' said Vi, looking at Mum as she high-kicked again, missing Mr Tilsley by a millimetre as he judo-rolled around the floor.

'What are we going to do?' Vi asked urgently.

'We need to stop the radio waves transmitting – we need a signal jammer,' said Russell. 'I might be able to make one. But I'll need something that transmits, like a remote control.'

'The AV table,' said Vi, pointing to the back of the hall. 'There's one for the projector. I'll get it.'

'OK,' said Russell, pulling tools and bits of circuitry out of his backpack. He was such a geek. But a useful one.

As Vi made her way to the AV table, she watched her mum wrestling Mr Tilsley by the broken buffet. Around the room, Henry Watts's mum was ninja-kicking the vaulting horse and Bessie Coates's dad was trying to chop one of the dinner tables in half. Vi grabbed the remote and scuttled back to Russell.

'Will this work?' she asked.

'I don't know,' Russell sighed, pulling the remote to pieces.

'I'll try to stop the music,' said Vi, crawling towards the DJ. 'Follow me.'

They scurried one table over and Vi took aim at the DJ. She set her Eye-Spy to one o'clock: tranquillizer darts.

'Sorry, Cheesy Ches,' whispered Vi, shooting the dart into his neck. 'Your set's over.'

She fired the dart and the DJ sank to the floor. Vi took his iPad from the deck.

'Shut it down,' said Russell.

'I can't,' said Vi. 'It's locked, I don't have the passcode. But wait – the song's changing . . .'

'What is it?' asked Russell, pulling wires out of the remote.

Vi grimaced.

'It's called . . . "Hit Me With Your Rhythm Stick",' she said grimly.

They peered over the DJ decks. Mrs Watts was attacking Mindy with a breadstick. Mr Coates was tickling Mrs Patel with a feather duster – although she seemed to be enjoying it. And Easter was approaching Mr Tilsley with the caretaker's broom. Vi looked at her watch. They'd already had over two minutes. The parents wouldn't be able to withstand much more from the Neurotrol.

'Noooooo!' cried Mr Tilsley, as Easter brandished the broom in front of him.

'Susan!' wailed Mindy as she tried to run from Mrs Watts while chasing Mr Coates with a baguette. 'What are you doing?'

Vi looked around at the chaos. The Neurotrol was controlling them all.

'Hurry up,' she hissed at Russell.

'I'm going as fast as I can,' he said, doing . . . something with a circuit board.

'The song's changing again,' said Vi. 'This one's slower. It's called . . . "Honesty".'

'What's happening?' wailed Mindy as Easter dropped the broom.

'I'll tell you what's happening,' said Easter. 'Your disco is rubbish, your buffet is cheap and those sausage rolls smell like compost!'

'Wow,' winced Vi.

'How dare you?' the PTA chair screamed as Mrs Watts declared that she'd added six books to her daughter's reading record and Mr Coates confessed to hiring a personal trainer for a year to win the dads' race on sports day. 'I never liked you anyway.'

'Maud!' Mr Tilsley yelled. 'I have something to tell you. Your sausage rolls – they're DISGUSTING!'

'YOU WHAT?' screamed Mrs Tilsley, storming over in her red jumpsuit. 'I knew I should have married your brother!'

'Susan . . . you need to . . . you need to . . .' Mindy cried as the song changed again.

'I'll tell you what I need to do,' Easter said, grabbing Mr Tilsley from his wife. 'I need to *Get Down with the Boogie*!'

'Whoooooaaaaa!' cried Mr Tilsley as Easter threw him in the air and caught him by his ankle, spinning him around like an ice skater. The dancing parents all turned to watch and soon Easter was at the heart of a circle as she spun Mr Tilsley up and down by his feet in a figure of eight, while Mrs Watts and Mr Coates held a dance-off next to the serving hatch.

'Go, Susan! Go, Susan! Go, go, go, Susan!' all the parents panted, boogieing to the point of collapse as Easter started swinging Mr Tilsley above her head.

'SHE'S GOING TO KILL ME!' Mr Tilsley cried.

'No, I'm not!' shrieked a frenzied Easter.

'I'm not talking about you,' shouted Mr Tilsley, looking very green. 'I'm talking about Maud! Don't let me go!'

Vi felt the panic sicken. Her mum was out of control. All the parents were. She watched as Easter swung poor Mr Tilsley around her head, her eyes wide and wild as the Neurotrol took hold. They'd all had enough. They were all going to explode. Vi would just have to go out there and take it from her mum. Russell's device clearly hadn't—

'Got it!' said Russell, snapping the last piece of his . . . messy wire thingy together.

'Will it work?' Vi asked.

'Let's find out,' said Russell, holding up his creation. 'Here goes.'

He slammed his finger on the volume button. It was as if the remote had switched the parents off. They all stopped dancing and stood panting in the middle of the room. Easter immediately released Mr Tilsley, who spun off across the room and landed on top of the basketball hoop.

'I don't know how long this will last,' said Russell, his home-made device crumbling in his hands. 'You need to get the Neurotrol and shut it down.'

He was right. And there was only one way of doing it. Now was the time for the bravest thing she'd ever done. Vi took a deep breath and crawled out from under the table.

'Mum!' she called, running over to Easter.

'Valentine?' she puffed, confused. 'What are you doing here?'

'I just . . . I just really needed a hug,' said Vi, throwing her arms around her mother and deftly lifting the Neurotrol out of her back pocket.

'What . . . what . . . what have I done?' Easter asked, looking at Mr Tilsley clinging on to the hoop as Mrs T pelted him with sausage rolls. 'Mindy, I'm so—'

'Please,' said Mindy, holding up a hand dramatically. 'Just leave.'

Gesturing to Russell to take Easter's other arm, Vi started to lead her mother out of the hall.

'And, Susan?' screamed Mindy as they made their way slowly back to the car. 'You can forget about the PTA summer barn dance!'

CHAPTER 15

'Now, today's trip to Dulworth Cove is an excellent opportunity to put our learning about coastal erosion into action,' said Mr Sprout excitedly over the coach's microphone the next morning, waking Vi up five minutes before the end of the bus journey she'd slept through. She'd spent a sleepless night worrying about the Neurotrol, convinced that Umbra would break in and steal it from her. Through the night, she'd hidden it under her pillow (too obvious), the oven (too dangerous) and the downstairs toilet (too gross). Should she just hand it over to SPIDER and take the consequences?

But her instincts told her no. The Cardinal's threat had been very clear – and besides, a top governmental spy agency wasn't likely to admit that they'd been outfoxed by an eleven-year-old girl to help her school application. She couldn't go to Rimmington Hall if she was in prison. The house was too risky with SPIDER sniffing around – so she'd decided to keep the Neurotrol with her today, then go straight to Autumn Leaves after school to get Nan to help her take it to Rimmington Hall. That was her best bet. Now if she could just have another five minutes' sleep . . .

'Can everyone check they have their water bottles?' Mr Sprout said brightly, rousing Vi from her doze. 'Hydration is super-important. Did you know that your brain is ninety-five per cent water? So make sure it doesn't get thirsty.'

Vi reached sleepily into her bag. But rather than finding her water bottle, the corner of an envelope scratched her fingertips. She pulled it out. It was a letter. And it was addressed to her.

She looked around – had that been in there when she'd left home this morning? Curiosity shook her out of her daze and she opened it.

Vi,

Forgive the old-fashioned note – strangely in these high-tech times, a letter can often be the most secure means of communication.

I know you must have a lot of questions and, Valentine, I am desperate to answer them. But I also know you have the Neurotrol. You are in extreme danger – and so am I. It is imperative you return it to me. To write more here could make a bad situation worse, but please – please – you have to trust me.

You must give me the Neurotrol. I only just got you back, my darling girl. I can't bear the thought of losing you again. I promise I can explain everything. And Robert Ford never breaks his promises.

Forever your daddy,
Robert

P.S. Great job with SPIDER last night. You're absolutely right not to trust them. You shouldn't trust anyone. Sorry for spying, but what can I say – old habits die hard xxx

Vi read the letter again. She didn't get it. Her father seemed so sincere – and all her instincts said to trust him. But this was a man who had fooled the world for years. He stole the Neurotrol. What was to say he wasn't fooling her too?

'Right – here we are,' said Mr Sprout. 'Everyone take a worksheet – I want you to find an example of each kind of erosion. But, remember, you are to stay with your partners at ALL times. The tides move very quickly here. Do not enter the caves directly, as you can easily become cut off. Now, find your partner.'

Vi watched as her classmates enthusiastically embraced their partners. She looked unenthusiastically at hers.

'Russell,' she sighed. 'Where shall we—'

'Oh Em Gee!' came Sally's cackle behind them. 'What *is* he wearing?'

'It's Sprout the Trout,' said Tom, winking at Vi. 'Looks like a fisherman, smells like a fish.'

'You heard my dad,' said Russell from deep within his waterproof everything, complete with a life ring slung over his shoulder. 'It's dangerous here.'

'Yeah,' said Sally. 'Major risk of crimes against fashion. Waterproofs are soooo out. Catch you later, Vi?'

'Sure,' said Vi, smiling weakly as the twins scuttled off. 'Come on, let's get this done. We'll go over there.'

'Is it safe?' Russell asked.

'It's a beach,' scoffed Vi. 'How dangerous can it be?'

'Very,' said Russell simply.

Vi skimmed over the long list of things they had to find.

'Look,' she whispered. 'This is going to be much quicker if we split up.'

'We're not allowed,' Russell insisted. 'You heard Dad.'

'Oh, will you shut up?' Vi snapped, her lack of sleep getting the better of her. 'You're always here, always under my feet – everywhere I turn. You're in my house, you're in my school – just . . . just leave me alone!'

Russell looked at her as though he'd been punched.

'Fine,' he said, shuffling away. 'Be careful.'

'*You* be careful,' muttered Vi.

Without her partner – and now in a foul mood – Vi stropped away to the other side of the bay. She didn't care what Mr Sprout said. She needed to be on her own.

She found a cave and climbed up to a ledge above its shallow rockpool with her worksheet.

But coastal erosion was the last thing on her mind. As she sat in a silent grump, she thought about her parents and about the Neurotrol, about Russell and Mr Sprout and Tom and Sally's party. Everything felt difficult and unfair. She didn't want to save the world right now. She just wanted her world to go back to normal. She took the Neurotrol out of her bag. It was so . . . ordinary. How could one stupid little thing cause such a fuss?

In frustration, she kicked the big stone next to her. But instead of landing on the sand beyond, it made a big plop as it landed in the water. She heard the roar of a jet-ski. How was it that close?

Vi looked up. She'd completely lost track of time and the tide was coming in. She'd better get back to the group before she—

'Valentine Day.'

Her distorted name echoed in the darkness as the familiar dark figure stood up on the jet ski.

'What are you doing here?' she said, looking nervously at the rising water.

'Give me the Neurotrol,' Umbra demanded, inching closer.

Vi's heart started to race. She reached for her

empty wrist – in her tiredness, she'd forgotten to put on her Eye-Spy. This was not good.

'Stay where you are,' she warned, backing into the cave. Umbra had come for the Neurotrol. Umbra had come for her.

Vi looked at the device in her hand. Should she use it? With the Neurotrol, she could control Umbra, make the super-villain do whatever she wanted. She could even rid the world of Umbra entirely . . .

But the thought quickly evaporated. Vi was ready to be a spy. She wasn't ready to be a killer. The Neurotrol robbed people of their free will and risked killing them. If she used it, she was no better than Umbra. She needed to do this the right way.

But the tide was coming in fast and Umbra was blocking her only, rapidly disappearing, way out. Vi was trapped. It was painful to admit it to herself, but she should have listened to Russell.

'I won't ask again,' Umbra threatened. 'Give me the Neurotrol.'

'One more millimetre and I'll scream,' said Vi, feeling the rising tide lap at her feet. Umbra ignored her, dismounting the jet-ski and jumping nimbly on to Vi's ledge.

'Then you'll get a very sore throat. This is not a game, little girl!' Umbra commanded. 'If you know what's good for you, you'll hand over the Neurotrol. Now.'

Vi kept walking backwards, but she was running out of ledge. The masked villain waded towards her. She was going to be caught. And then ... She dreaded to think what then. This was what her mum had been worrying about all these years. This was what she'd been trying to protect her from. No wonder Easter couldn't chill ...

'There's no way out, Valentine,' Umbra continued. 'Hand it over and I might let you live.'

Vi looked around desperately. She'd been stupid. She'd let her determination to prove she could be a spy put her life in danger. If she ever got out of this, she'd do things differently. She'd ask for help. She'd listen to her mother. She'd ...

She'd do *something*. Probably.

Umbra was right upon her. She could see her terrified reflection in Umbra's mask, the intersecting circles marked on her forehead. A gloved hand reached towards her. Any second now she'd be in its grasp ...

Suddenly, a small metal object flew out of nowhere and landed on the back of Umbra's mask. The moment it made contact, Umbra began shaking uncontrollably.

'W-w-what the . . .' Umbra burbled, wobbling around and teetering on the brink of the ledge.

Vi had no idea what just happened. But she wasn't going to waste it.

Your environment can be your best weapon, she remembered Siren saying. *Make sure you use it . . .*

Vi looked at the waves below.

'Umbra?' she asked.

'W-w-w-what?' spluttered the villain.

'I hope you're a good swimmer!' Vi roared, and gave Umbra an almighty shove. The cloaked figure swayed on the edge of the ledge, looking for a moment as though balance could be found. But gravity had other ideas. With a heavy splash, Umbra plunged into the water below. The waves pulled the hooded figure down before spewing it back up several metres away.

'No!' spluttered Umbra. 'I want my Neurotrol! Valentine Day! I'm going to—'

But whatever Umbra was threatening was washed away by the tide. The water whisked the villain out of the cave, past the jet-ski and out to the wider sea.

That was one problem taken care of – but as Vi looked at the few remaining centimetres of ledge, she had another one. A big one. The tide was rising with each second – soon there'd be no ledge to stand on. She considered her sole option. She was a good swimmer. If she could just get to the jet-ski, perhaps she could shout for help. The masked figure wasn't prepared for the water. She was. She could do this. And as the water rose, she had no choice.

She took out a towel and wrapped the Neurotrol tight inside before putting the bundle inside a plastic bag in her backpack.

'Let's hope we're both waterproof,' she said, looking at the deep water below. This was possibly the stupidest thing she'd ever done. And she'd once tried to pierce her own ears with a cocktail stick.

Vi put on the bag. She took a deep breath, pinched her nose and jumped into the sea. But before she could even resurface the tide had got hold of her and was sweeping her away. It was so strong, pulling her under and further out to sea with each wave. There was nothing she could do.

She wasn't that far from the beach – but the current was acting against her and refusing to let her get near it. She whooshed past the jet-ski – any moment she'd be in the open sea. And then she'd . . .

Something landed on the water in front of her. It was a life ring. The salty water was obscuring her vision. But she knew it was her only chance to stay afloat.

The ring was just a few metres ahead of her. Vi tried to swim towards it. The current was just too strong. She took a deep breath. She could do this. She had to do this. The ring was right there. All she needed to do was take two massive strokes towards it. She gritted her teeth, put her head down and swam with all her might, reaching out for the ring that could save her life . . .

'Gotcha,' she spluttered as her fingers made contact. She pulled herself on to the ring and felt it being dragged towards the shore. She choked as she took in a big mouthful of salt water. As she coughed it out, she felt her feet make contact with the sand. She clambered out of the ring and on to the beach. She was safe. But who did she have to thank?

'Russell?' she said in disbelief at the anxious face of her nearly-stepbrother. 'Is that you?'

'I looked for you everywhere,' said Russell, sounding genuinely scared. 'When I saw Umbra in the cove . . .'

Vi lay back on the sand. She was OK. She held a hand to her head. Shame she couldn't say the same about her hair.

'What was that . . . thing you threw?' she asked.

'Ah,' smiled Russell, pulling a small silver ball out of his bag. 'That'll be an electroblaster. I designed them for BlitzBotz – they release electrical current upon detonation. Looks like they work.'

'Nice shot,' smiled Vi.

'Years of being a goal post in PE teaches you a lot about angles and trajectories,' smiled Russell. 'Are you OK?'

'I'm fine,' shivered Vi. 'Bit cold. But fine.'

She suddenly panicked – the Neurotrol. She unpacked her rucksack and opened the soggy plastic bag. The towel was damp. But the Neurotrol was dry.

'When I saw you, I thought you were going to . . . Vi . . . this is too much. You could have died.'

'I know,' said Vi. 'And . . . I'm sorry for what I said before. I'm . . . I'm really glad you were here.'

'You're welcome,' said Russell with a shy smile. 'And, look – I've got spare uniform in my bag. Even Dad might notice you're soaking wet.'

'Thanks,' said Vi, accepting the dry clothes and the towel they were wrapped in. She dried off the Neurotrol and switched it on. The light went on. It still worked.

'We'd better go,' said Russell, as Vi got to her feet. 'What are you going to do?'

Vi let out a deep breath as she switched the Neurotrol off and put it in her bag. She'd been lucky this time. But this was getting seriously dangerous. Umbra had attacked her twice in a few days. She didn't know if she could rely on her dad, she could get into huge trouble with SPIDER and she was an eleven-year old girl carrying a device that could control the adult population of the planet. Who could she trust?

The answer came back as quickly and as clearly as a ringing bell. There was one person she could always trust. The one person who had always kept her safe. The one person she should have listened to. The one person she needed more than anyone right now.

'I have to talk to my mum,' said Vi. 'I have to tell her everything. She'll know what to do.'

'Finally,' sighed Russell. 'Let's go.'

Vi nodded as she shivered in her towel. Everything would be fine. She just needed to get home. She just needed to get to her mum.

And once she'd told Easter everything she'd been up to, she just needed to get as big a head start as humanly possible.

CHAPTER 16

After a long journey, with Vi far too wired to sleep this time, the coach pulled up at school and everyone filed out for their parents to collect them. The Sprouts had another practice match planned after school, so Vi would have a chance to talk to her mum alone. Vi looked urgently for Easter's car. But Easter wasn't there. She was always the first parent at the gates. Where was she?

Out of the corner of her eye, Vi saw Tom and Sally slither over from the other side of the playground.

'So, Vi,' said Tom, looking directly at Vi over his shades. Those eyes didn't seem quite as lovely as she remembered them. 'Our parents have hired us a limo to go to BlitzBotz on Saturday. We've only got eight seats. Do you want one?'

'Um, sure,' she said, looking around them to double-check Easter wasn't in the crowd of waiting parents.

'Wow. So uninterested,' whispered Sally. 'That's soooo in. We'll pick you up from your place on Saturday morning?'

'Great,' said Vi distractedly. 'See you then.'

She looked to the gates again. Her mum was never this late – what was going on?

'Oh, you are kidding me,' she heard Tom drawl, signalling to the corner of the playground where Russell was playing with Agadoo. 'The Freak's got a friend.'

'Is that his BlitzBot?' Sally asked. 'It actually looks quite good.'

'Not for long,' said Tom. He might have had nice eyes. But he had a really cruel smile. 'Follow me.'

Vi felt the panic rise in her stomach. She couldn't handle this right now, she had bigger problems.

'Um . . . just leave him, he's not worth your time,' she tried to say casually.

'Oh, this will be,' said Sally, mirroring her brother's evil grin as they approached Russell. 'Believe me.'

'Sprouty,' said Tom, taking off his shades and pulling his water bottle out of his backpack.

'What do you want?' said Russell, standing protectively in front of Agadoo.

'Nice bot,' said Sally.

'Leave me alone,' said Russell. 'My dad will be back in a minute, he's just picking up his marking.'

'Well, that's not very friendly!' said Tom, taking a big swig from his bottle. 'We're only admiring your robot.'

'Well, don't,' said Russell, looking for support from Vi.

Vi jiggled on the spot. Where was Easter? If she turned up now, all this would go away.

She moved her hand gently to her Eye-Spy – it still wasn't there. She remembered Nan's warning about never leaving home without it. She vowed to start listening to what adults were telling her. Sometimes.

'Are you thirsty?' Tom asked, offering Russell the water bottle.

'No. Thank you,' said Russell firmly.

'I wasn't asking you,' said Tom, moving the bottle. 'I was asking your bot. Do you think he looks thirsty, Sal?'

'Very thirsty,' said Sal. 'You know what Mr Sprout told us – the human brain is ninety-five per cent water . . .'

'That must be why he's so wet,' Tom grinned, shaking the bottle and spilling some drops near Agadoo.

'I'm thirsty,' said Vi, desperately trying to find her mum in the dwindling group of parents. 'Can I have a drink?'

'Wait your turn,' smiled Tom, tipping the bottle towards Agadoo.

'Don't you dare,' said Russell through gritted teeth.

'Sal?' Tom commanded.

Sal came forward and pushed Russell to the floor.

'Silly me,' she said, raising her hand to her lips. 'I'm such a klutz.'

'OK, let's all calm down,' said Vi unevenly. 'My mum will be here any second . . .'

'Ooooops!' said Tom, holding the bottle over Agadoo. 'Looks like you're not the only klutz, Sal.'

And with that, he emptied the entire bottle over Agadoo.

'No!' cried Russell, reaching out a hand to stop Tom. But it was too late. As Agadoo sparked and crackled and fizzed while playing a weird song about doing the Superman, Tom shook the final drops out of his bottle.

'There,' said Tom, screwing the lid back on his bottle. 'Much, much better.'

Russell and Vi looked in horror at the smouldering Agadoo.

'You . . . you . . . IDIOT!' screamed Russell, incandescent with rage. He leapt off the floor and charged at Tom, knocking him to the ground and slapping him with all his might.

'Argh! Argh! Not the face! I have a party!' Tom squealed. 'Saaaaaaalllllll!'

Sally clenched her fists and emitted a scream so loud it brought everyone to a standstill.

A whistle went off over the other side of the playground.

'Stop that! Stop!' called Mr Sprout, rushing over to the fray. He pulled Russell off Tom and stared at him in disbelief. 'Russ? What are you . . .'

Russell shrugged him off and wiped his face. Vi could see tears. She didn't know if they were angry or sad. But there were lots of them.

'What is the meaning of this?' said Mr Sprout, aghast.

'He attacked me, sir!' Tom squealed. 'I accidentally spilt some of my water – because hydration is super-important – on his stupid toy and he went ballistic!'

'Russell?' Mr Sprout asked. 'Is this true?'

Russell said nothing. He just stood and stared at the motionless Agadoo, still dripping and sparking on the tarmac.

'OK,' said Mr Sprout. 'We need to talk to Mrs Hasan. Fighting is against the school rules – and the rules apply to everyone. Come with me, you two.'

Russell and Tom followed Mr Sprout into the school, with Sally yapping behind like an irritating puppy. Vi watched them go with a heavy heart. Russell was in huge trouble – fighting was strictly forbidden. He'd be lucky not to be excluded.

Vi walked over to Agadoo. He was still wet from Tom's water bottle, so she took off Russell's replacement jumper and tried to dry him off – maybe if he wasn't wet he might work?

But it was no use. Agadoo was dead. She looked up at the gates. All the parents had gone. Easter wasn't there. There was no one to help her.

'I'm so sorry,' she whispered as she picked Agadoo up and carried him across the playground. 'I'll make this right. I promise.'

'I don't understand it!' said Mr Sprout in the car. Easter still hadn't arrived after Russell's visit to Mrs Hasan. Agadoo couldn't fight in the practice match, so Mr Sprout was driving everyone home. 'Fighting? That's just . . . that's so not you, Russ.'

Russell said nothing, but stayed silently slumped against the car door.

'Er, Mr Sprout – have you spoken to Mum today?' Vi asked anxiously. Something wasn't right. Her mum never forgot to pick her up from school.

'No,' said Mr Sprout distractedly. 'Russell, you do realize that this suspension means you can kiss goodbye to your scholarship to the Tech Academy?'

This shocked Vi out of her own worries for a moment. If Russell couldn't go to the Tech Academy, he'd have to go to St Michael's. With Tom and Sally. It would be miserable for him. That was really unfair. Why wasn't Russell speaking up for himself?

'Why would you do this?' exclaimed Mr Sprout. 'Why ruin everything you've worked for, why?'

'Tom and Sally broke Agadoo,' said Vi, saying what Russell would not. 'On purpose.'

'Is that what all this is about?' said Mr Sprout. 'We'll fix him, Russ, we've done it enough times before.'

'They poured a whole bottle of water on him,' Russell sniffed. 'All his electrics are fried. There's no way we'll fix that by Saturday.'

Mr Sprout let out a long sigh. Vi looked out of the windscreen. They were nearly home. Mum would be there and she would make everything better. Why was this car journey taking so long?

'Well, clearly I need to have another chat with Mrs Hasan,' said Mr Sprout. 'That kind of destructive behaviour is totally unacceptable.'

'Doesn't make any difference to Agadoo,' said Russell, his eyes starting to fill. 'We still won't be able to do BlitzBotz.'

'There's always next year, Russ – we'll make him even better,' Mr Sprout assured him.

'I don't want to do it next year!' Russell cried. 'I want to do it this year. With you. And Agadoo. And Mum.'

He started to sob into his knees as they pulled into the driveway.

'Vi,' said Mr Sprout softly. 'Would you give us a minute?'

'Sure,' said Vi, springing out of the car to the sound of Russell's tears. She felt terrible. She would make this right. Just as soon as she had talked to Mum.

Vi went to find her keys, but was surprised to find the door slightly ajar. That wasn't like Mum, she was super-paranoid about security. What was she—

'Mum?' Vi called, a knot of fear tightening in her stomach as she pushed the door open.

But one look at the house gave her all the answers she needed. Everything had been trashed – furniture, paintings, plants – there had been a massive struggle in here.

'Mum?' she called desperately, searching through the rooms. 'Mum?'

Easter wasn't there. There was an envelope on the kitchen table, though. And on it, the unmistakable mark of two circles joined by intersecting lines. The darkest part of a shadow.

'Umbra,' Vi whispered. She tore the envelope open. It was a simple message. With a terrifying meaning.

VALENTINE DAY,

THANK YOU SO MUCH FOR MY REFRESHING DIP TODAY. I HOPE TO RETURN THE FAVOUR SOON.

YOU HAVE TAKEN SOMETHING OF MINE, SO I HAVE TAKEN SOMETHING OF YOURS. MEET ME AT THE NORTON POWER STATION WITH THE NEUROTROL IF YOU WANT TO SEE YOUR PARENTS ALIVE. ALERT THE AUTHORITIES AND YOU ALL DIE TODAY.

UMBRA

She heard Mr Sprout and Russell walk into the hall.

'What on earth—' Mr Sprout began as he saw the carnage. Vi took a deep breath. This time, no amount of lying was going to hide the truth.

'Mr Sprout,' she said soothingly. 'You should sit down. There are a few things you need to know.'

CHAPTER 17

All things considered, George Sprout was taking the news pretty well.

'So . . .' he began for the hundredth time, 'that time your mum jumped on board a moving speedboat when we took that river cruise in London was because . . .'

'She used to be a spy, Agent Lynx,' Vi answered for the hundred-and-first time as they waited in St Xavier's car park. 'She spotted a known weapons smuggler by the London Eye. She wasn't just worried about the effects of water vehicles on marine wildlife.'

'Oh,' said Mr Sprout, looking genuinely confused. 'Vi, I really think this is a matter for the authorities, your parents could be in serious danger.'

'They'll be in even more danger if we get the police involved,' said Vi. 'You read the note. We have to do this ourselves.'

'Well, it sounds very risky,' said Mr Sprout. 'I'm not at all happy at the idea of two kids and one middle-aged schoolteacher taking on this Umbra.'

Vi looked at Russell in the back seat. He hadn't said much during the journey, apart from insisting he come too and Vi was glad – Russell had proven useful before. Vi was less convinced that Mr Sprout would be. But he was the only one with a driving licence.

'We're not just two kids and a middle-aged schoolteacher,' said Vi as a van with *Auguste's Balloon Animals* written on the side screeched into the car park next to them. 'We have help.'

The van door opened to the sound of soft saxophone music. A long, PVC-clad leg emerged, followed swiftly by the rest of Siren in a red PVC catsuit.

'Wow,' gasped Mr Sprout as they got out of the car. 'That's Siren. I used to have posters of her all over my wall . . . I'm a huge fan.'

'Don't let Mum hear you say that,' warned Vi.

'Hey,' said Siren. 'Nice to meet you.'

'You too,' said Mr Sprout enthusiastically. 'Did you know that German chemist Eugen Baumann accidentally discovered PVC in 1872. He discovered the polymer—'

'—inside a flask of vinyl chloride which had been left in the sunlight,' Siren added with a smile. 'It's flexible, durable and fire-resistant. It's just a shame it gets so warm. It's like the inside of a mouldy welly in here.'

'Hey guys,' Vi said, as Auguste and Dr Doppelganger piled out behind Siren. 'Thanks for coming.'

'Of course,' said Dr D's right head, eyeing up a bemused Mr Sprout. 'At EVIL, we're all for one and one for all.'

'And with us – you get two for one,' said his left head. 'Now where is Umbra? I'm ready to kick some—'

Two bats flew into the car park, one immediately turning into Dimitri, the other remaining as Nigel.

'Wow – there's a very negative energy here,' said Dimitri. 'I wonder if now would be a good time for some positive affirmations?'

‘’Oo do we kill first?’ grinned Auguste, clicking his clown umbrella in a way that sounded suspiciously like a gun.

Nigel the bat squeaked a laugh.

‘Please, Nigel, don’t enable his patriarchal aggression,’ whispered Dimitri.

‘Valentine?’ whispered Mr Sprout out of the corner of his mouth. ‘How do you know these . . . people?’

‘They’re friends of my dad’s,’ Vi explained.

‘Of course they are,’ nodded Mr Sprout. ‘I suppose he’s a spy too?’

‘Not exactly,’ Vi continued. ‘He is . . . was . . . maybe . . . a super-villain. It’s complicated.’

‘Of course it is,’ Mr Sprout sighed.

‘OK,’ said Vi. ‘Dimitri has done some . . . Er, Dave, do you mind?’

Dave took his saxophone out of his mouth and moved slowly back into the van.

‘Thanks,’ said Vi, bringing Dimitri to the centre of the gathering. ‘Dimitri has done some surveillance on the power station so we know what we’re facing. Dimitri?’

‘Thank you,’ said the vampire earnestly. ‘But if anyone wants to chip in at any point, this is a free-flowing exchange of ideas where everyone's contribution is valid . . .'

'Move it along, toothy!' shouted Dr Doppelganger's left head.

'Robbed of my voice,' sighed Dimitri, picking up a piece of chalk and squatting on the car park floor. 'OK – from what I can tell, inside the compound there is one central column, here.'

He drew a rough outline of a tower on the floor.

'There is only one entrance, but it is heavily guarded.'

'Siren?' Vi smiled. 'Sounds like a job for you.'

'Got it,' winked Siren. 'Auguste, Dimitri, Doc – you're with me.'

'*Très bien*,' grinned Auguste. 'Now we can kill zem, no?'

'No,' said Vi. 'No . . . eliminating.'

Auguste's big red smile turned upside down.

'*Dommage*,' he huffed.

'The whole tower is rigged to explode,' Dimitri continued, adding a small box outside the tower. 'Everything is controlled by a computer system in this outbuilding, here. Who has technological expertise?'

The EVILs looked between one another.

'Don't look at me,' said Dr Doppelganger's right head. 'I'm a chemist.'

'You're an idiot,' said his left. 'Auguste – you know about this stuff?'

'*Mais non*,' shrugged Auguste, producing a large round bomb from his trouser pocket. 'I prefer ze old school.'

'Siren?' asked Vi.

'Sorry, kiddo,' Siren pouted. 'The only thing I can hack is a mucus cough.'

'I can do it,' came a small voice from the back of the group.

Everyone parted to reveal Russell hitching his glasses up his nose.

'No,' said Mr Sprout to his son. 'It's too dangerous. You—'

'I'm the only person who can help,' said Russell. 'It's fine, Dad. I've got this.'

'He's brilliant,' Vi said, smiling at her nearly-stepbrother. 'Trust him.'

Mr Sprout nodded reluctantly.

'He *is* brilliant,' said Mr Sprout. 'And I always trust him.'

Russell blushed slightly and shuffled his feet awkwardly.

'Where are my parents?' Vi asked Dimitri.

'They are in the tower,' he explained. 'I couldn't see them, but I could certainly hear them. Valentine, I should warn you. It's very dangerous in there.'

'I know,' said Vi. 'Umbra wants revenge and will stop at nothing.'

'No,' said Dimitri. 'I meant your parents. I heard some language that I must say I found very offensive – I wonder if they'd benefit from some couples' therapy . . .'

'They're not a couple,' said Mr Sprout defensively. 'Easter is my . . . fiancée.'

Vi and Russell exchanged a smile. That was encouraging.

'OK,' said Vi. 'Everyone know what they're doing? Good. George – our job is to find and rescue Mum and Dad . . .'

She stopped as Mr Sprout choked on a small sob.

'Are you OK?' she asked.

'Yes,' he sniffed.

'OK . . .' said Vi. That was weird. 'Everyone clear?'

The unlikely comrades nodded at least one of their heads.

'Um – here,' said Russell, pulling some gadgets out of his backpack. 'I made these walkie-talkies. They're pretty basic, but they should keep us in touch.'

'Great idea,' said Siren, ruffling his hair. 'Thanks, kid.'

Russell's blush went into full bloom as he looked straight at the floor.

'Good luck, everyone,' said Vi, taking her walkie-talkie. 'And thanks.'

EVIL piled back into their van as Vi and the Sprouts headed for the car.

'George?' Vi asked, an idea coming to her as she strapped on her seat belt. 'Please may I borrow your phone?'

'Sure,' said George, taking it out of his pocket. 'And, Vi?'

'Yes?' she said, checking the Eye-Spy she'd made sure to bring this time.

'I really like it when you call me George,' he smiled, putting his hand on hers.

She looked into the kindly eyes of her nearly-stepfather.

'So do I,' she smiled. 'Now let's go and save my parents.'

As Dimitri had told them, the sole entrance to Norton Power Station was heavily guarded. Vi counted ten masked henchmen standing outside with guns.

'How are we going to get past those guys?' George whispered as Russell pulled his laptop out.

'We don't,' she whispered back. 'Siren does. Come on – where is she?'

The soft sound of saxophone music answered her question.

'Oh, hi boys,' exhaled Siren, slinking towards the guards. 'I was just wondering if there was a ladies' I could use? Bit of an urgent toilet situation. Refried bean fajitas last night. I have a bum like a chocolate fountain.'

'Urghturblusrlubhshumph,' the first henchman replied. 'Erm . . . do you have a security pass?'

'Hmmm – let me see, I'm sure I had one in here somewhere . . .'

She started to pat around the catsuit, which had lots of things inside it, none of them pockets.

'She's quite something,' George sighed.

'Yes, she's very pretty,' droned Vi, rolling her eyes.

'Is she?' said George. 'Hadn't noticed. She's not a patch on your mum. But I was seriously impressed by her on *Mastermind*. She won twenty-five series. Would have been twenty-six if the trophy hadn't mysteriously disappeared.'

'Oh no,' said Siren, raising a finger to her bottom lip. 'I seem to have misplaced my pass. It was definitely there when I was plucking my nose hairs this morning. Perhaps I—'

SPLAT!

A large custard pie hit the first henchman straight in the face.

'Oi! he yelped. 'What the 'eck do you think you're— Tortoise . . . Unicorn . . . Middlesbrough . . .'

And with a soft splat, the henchman dropped to the floor. The other nine henchmen cocked their weapons. A mad laugh erupted across the car park.

'Zees is a funny joke, no?' Auguste giggled. 'Custard pies filled with sedatives! 'Eee will sleep like a tiny *bébé*! Now we kill him . . .'

'NO!' shouted the rest of EVIL, reaching for the clown's umbrella.

The henchmen opened fire and Auguste immediately opened the umbrella, creating a bulletproof shield around the EVILs. They waited until the henchmen needed to reload, then attacked them again with the sedative custard pies. Four of the guards were taken out, but five raised their weapons once more.

'Take that!' said Dr Doppelganger, hurling a flask containing a bubbling green liquid at them. It exploded at the feet of two of the henchmen, who immediately started shrinking, getting smaller and smaller until they were little babies running around naked outside the power station.

'Three to go,' said Vi as the remaining hench men advanced.

'I've got this,' said Dimitri, taking flight and drawing fire from the guards. He let out a high-pitched squeal that made the very ground shake.

'Ow!' cried Vi, slapping her hands over her ears. 'Russell – are you ready to make a run for it?'

'Just say the word,' said Russell, hitching his glasses up his nose.

At Dimitri's call, the sky suddenly darkened,

the air turning black with whatever dark magic he had summoned. But as the black cloud descended, it became clear that it wasn't magic at all – it was bats. Thousands and thousands of bats.

They swooped from the sky, attacking the last henchmen standing, hundreds of them descending until the men were forced to drop their weapons and run for cover, calling for back-up as they scattered.

'Cousin Vladimir, have you been working out?' Dimitri called out. 'Aunt Lucretia, 942 years young, I see . . .'

'All clear?' Vi called to Siren. 'Can you stay here and keep the back-up out?'

'We've got this, kiddo,' said the femme fatale, who had one of the baby henchmen asleep in her arms. 'Go and save your folks. Give your daddy a kiss from me. I would, but I haven't cleaned my teeth . . .'

'We won't let you down,' said Dr Doppelganger's right head as his left winked reassuringly.

'You are a strong, empowered young woman,' said Dimitri. 'We are proud to be your friends.'

'I'd still like to kill you,' said Auguste. 'But with ze utmost respect.'

'Er . . . thanks,' said Vi, as EVIL rounded up the henchmen. 'OK, Russell – go!'

Russell ran – well, as close as he ever got to running – across the empty car park into the small brick building containing the computer system. Vi watched through the sole window as he wired up his laptop and started jabbing at the keyboard.

'Russell?' said Vi over the walkie-talkie. 'Russell, can you hear me?'

'Copy that,' said Russell. 'I'm just trying to unlock the system and . . . I'm in. What do you need?'

'Open the main door,' said Vi, 'then get to work on that bomb.'

'Roger that,' said Russell as the door started to open.

'Are you ready?' she asked George Sprout.

'For anything,' said George, taking her hand.

They ran across the car park, skirting around the unconscious henchmen and into the entrance Russell had opened. Three corridors opened up in front of them.

'Argh!' she cried. 'I've no idea where to go – we don't have time to get this wrong. We need a map, a guide, a . . .'

'It's this one,' said Mr Sprout, heading off down the left-hand corridor. 'Did you know that this power station was built in 1933, to massive protests from the residents before it was decommissioned in 1978? The two ancillary towers were demolished in 1987, but this third one, which can only be accessed from the left corridor, was left in the hopes of future redevelopment.'

'No,' Vi smiled, running up the corridor. 'I didn't. But I'm glad you did.'

Mr Sprout grinned at her and pushed his glasses up his nose.

'Let's go,' said Vi, running into the darkness.

As they raced along the tunnel, they could hear shouting ahead.

'Where is it?' a menacing voice asked, followed by a sickening thud and a groan.

'I'm telling you,' came Robert's defiant voice, 'I don't have it.'

'My dad!' whispered Vi, rushing towards the voices. 'He's in trouble. Come on, George.'

'Vi, we need to proceed with extreme caution,' warned George as she raced ahead. But Vi wasn't listening. She charged down the corridor until they came to a large set of double doors, one of which was slightly ajar.

Vi peered through. There, bound and gagged and suspended high on a platform above a bubbling pool, was her mother, wrestling against her restraints. On the ground, Robert was tied to a chair. He was bleeding. And a huge, bald white henchman looked like the reason why.

'I'll ask you one more time,' growled the henchman pulling out a gun. 'Where is the Neurotrol?'

'And I'll answer one more time, you ignorant thug,' said Robert, 'I don't have it.'

'Well, then,' said the henchman, cocking his gun. 'You're no use to me. See you, Sir Charge . . .'

'Wait!' said Vi, charging through the doors. 'Don't shoot! I've got it – I've got the Neurotrol. See? It's right here.'

She pulled the phone out of her pocket and held it up for the henchman to see. She could hear Easter screaming through her gag.

'It's OK, Mum!' she shouted. 'Don't worry, I've come to rescue you.'

'Give me the Neurotrol,' said the henchman.

'If I do, you have to let my parents go,' said Vi.

'Vi – be careful,' said Mr Sprout behind her.

'I don't think you're in a position to be making

demands, shorty,' said the henchman. 'Hand it over, or I'll fill your dad so full of holes he'll be able to strain spaghetti.'

'Vi – don't give it to him,' said her dad. 'You can't trust anyone.'

Vi looked at her mum gnashing at her gag and the gun pointing at her dad. She knew exactly what she had to do.

'Here,' she said, tossing the phone to the henchman. 'You got what you wanted. Now let them go.'

'Vi – NO!' she heard her mum shout, finally free of the gag. 'Vi, don't – it's a trap! Robert told me Umbra had imprisoned you here! He's—'

'Sorry, sweetheart,' the henchman growled, picking up the phone. 'Not my call. Need to check with my boss.'

He looked at Robert, who calmly shook off his ropes, slicked back his hair, wiped what now appeared be ketchup off his face and stood up to rearrange his jacket.

'I work,' said the henchman, 'for Sir Charge.'

And with that, he handed the phone to Robert.

CHAPTER 18

'Thank you, Mick,' said Robert, accepting the Neurotrol from his henchman. 'I can take it from here. Great performance, by the way – loved the spaghetti line.'

'Thanks, boss,' said Mick in a rather higher and far posher voice. 'I knew that time in the Cambridge Footlights wouldn't be wasted.'

'I KNEW IT!' Vi shouted at her father as Mick grabbed George and pinned his arms behind his back. 'I knew I shouldn't have trusted you!'

'You should have listened to Daddy,' sighed Robert. 'I warned you not to trust anyone.'

'You leave Vi out of this!' Easter screamed, pulling at the ropes that were tying her to the platform. 'It's me Umbra wants! This has nothing to do with her!'

'I'm afraid it has everything to do with her,' Robert said coolly. 'She's been interfering with our plans for days. And now it's time for her to stop.'

Vi reached slowly for her Eye-Spy. But Robert spotted it and snapped his hand over her wrist.

'I'll be taking that, thank you,' he said, unstrapping it. He put it in his suit pocket and tapped it with a satisfied wink.

'What are you doing?' screamed Easter. 'A young girl has no place here!'

'I think you'll find—' Robert began.

'I wasn't talking to you!' Easter snapped. 'I meant you, Valentine Day! What are you *thinking* getting mixed up in all this?'

'I . . . er . . . I kinda . . .'

'What did you expect, Bunny?' Robert began.

'MY NAME IS SUSAN!' Easter raged.

'Well, whoever you are, Valentine is our daughter,' Robert shot back. 'She was never going to sit on the sidelines. Even if, on this occasion, she should have done.'

'You stay out of this!' Easter snapped. 'This is all your fault – everything was fine before you came along.'

The room filled with the sound of a distorted, deep laugh coming from the speakers around the wall. A big screen flickered to life and a now all-too-familiar masked face filled it.

'Everything's under control, boss,' said Robert. 'As you can see, I have secured the Neurotrol and Easter Day. Come and get them.'

'On my way. Dear, dear, dear,' Umbra tutted, above the chunter of helicopter blades. 'Trouble in paradise? You two used to be such lovebirds.'

'Well, not any more!' Easter screamed. 'We're divorced.'

'Not technically,' Robert smirked.

'If you say one more word . . .!' Easter shrieked.

As her parents squabbled, Vi looked around the room. Was there anything she could use? Anything at all to help her mum escape? Anything to shut the pair of them up?

'Easter Day,' Umbra began again. 'Last time we were in a deserted power station, you tried to kill me. Now we're all here again and I'm *actually* going to kill you.'

'Let her go,' said Vi, trying to keep the tremble out of her voice.

'Oh dear, little one,' said Umbra. 'You still don't

understand the rules, do you? I have the Neurotrol and your mother. You're not in the best position to negotiate.'

'Not exactly,' said Vi, pulling something out of her backpack. 'You do have my mother. But you also have George's mobile phone.'

'Er . . . I'll be needing that back,' whispered George. 'Did you know that mobile phones now have more computing power than the computers used for the Apollo 11 moon landings?'

'Is that so?' said Mick with genuine interest. 'Well, I never.'

Vi looked smugly at Robert as she held the real Neurotrol over the tank. She looked inside. It was full of snapping mutant piranhas. Of course it was. The mutant fish were all shapes and sizes – some had three eyes, some had legs – at least one had the rear end of a cow.

'Oh, now that's clever,' said Mick admiringly. 'Well played.'

'You see,' Vi said to Robert as she dangled the Neurotrol over the fish. 'I did take your advice, Daddy. I don't trust you at all. Now, Umbra, let my mum go or you can kiss your precious Neurotrol goodbye. And you can kiss my butt while you're there.'

'I have to hand it to you, Vi,' said Robert, approaching slowly. She could hear him trying to control his breath. She'd got to him. 'You're plucky.'

'Don't encourage her,' Easter scolded. 'And you watch your mouth, young lady.'

'But . . . Umbra's the baddie!'

'I raised you properly,' chided Easter. 'Mind your Ps and Qs.'

Vi waggled the Neurotrol over the piranhas again as Robert approached.

'One more step and the piranhas get lunch,' she threatened.

'And your mother will be dessert,' Robert said gravely. 'Don't do it, Vi.'

'If I may interrupt,' Umbra announced. 'Miss Day, unless you hand over the Neurotrol, I'm going to lower your mother into the pit of piranhas below.'

'So old school,' Robert murmured admiringly.

'How do I know you won't do it anyway?' Vi shouted.

Umbra laughed softly.

'You don't. But I don't see you have a great deal

of choice. Now give him the Neurotrol.'

'No,' said Vi firmly, before looking at her mother. 'Thank you.'

'I see,' said Umbra. 'Then I suggest you say farewell to Mummy.'

The platform suddenly dropped, sending the piranhas below into a frenzy. The tower filled with the sound of Easter's screams. Vi watched in horror as her mum plummeted towards the frothing tank . . .

'STOP!' Vi shouted just before Easter hit the water. 'OK, OK – I'll give you the Neurotrol.'

'Valentine – no!' Easter shouted, as she was winched slowly back up to safety. 'With that technology, Umbra can control the minds of billions of people all over the world! They'll be powerless to resist and could be forced to do anything – war, assassinations . . .'

'PTA events?' Robert suggested.

'I'm not worth it, Vi,' Easter pleaded.

Vi looked at her mum. The woman who had kept her safe. Who was still trying to keep the world safe. Who was just incredibly awesome.

'Yes, you are,' Vi insisted. 'You're my world.'

Vi looked up at the screen.

'Umbra?' she said. 'Take it. It's yours.'

She tossed the Neurotrol at Robert's feet. He pulled out the side and checked the microchip within. He held it up to the light, replaced it in the phone and breathed a deep sigh of relief. His eyes locked with hers for a moment. Was he trying to tell her something? If he was, he didn't want to hear her reply . . .

Vi bowed her head. She'd failed her mission. She'd failed the world. And she'd failed at being a spy.

There was a brief silence, filled all too soon with a satisfied laugh.

'Thank you, Valentine,' said Umbra. 'I'm very grateful. So grateful, in fact, I'm going to reunite you with your family . . .'

Vi looked at George and breathed a sigh of relief. It was going to be OK.

'. . . by putting you all in the tank together,' Umbra continued. 'I told you I owed you a dip. Sir Charge? Let's kill three birds with one stone.'

Robert hesitated, looking at Vi. Was that . . . fear in his eyes?

'Why don't you come here and do it yourself?' Robert asked. 'It's been a while.'

'Do not question my orders again!' Umbra roared. 'Take the child and put her in the tank with her mother. Unless, of course, you want to join them?'

'Of course not,' said Robert smoothly. 'It will be my pleasure.'

Robert walked slowly over to Vi and tied her hands behind her back.

'Get off me, you freak!' she raged, struggling against him.

'Valentine, don't struggle,' said Robert, looking her squarely in the eyes. 'You'll just make it worse.'

He held her ropes and she and George were forced higher and higher up the flight of metal stairs towards Easter on the platform. Vi wrestled against her father's strong grip, but he held her tight. When they reached the top, Mick pushed George down and tied his hands behind the pole. Robert was taking his time to do Vi's. She saw her Eye-Spy hanging out of his pocket. If she could just . . .

'No!' she suddenly shouted, jumping up and grabbing Robert. 'I won't let you, I won't!'

She jabbed her hand into his pocket, pulled out her watch and putpocketed it into the back of her jeans.

'Valentine!' Robert said firmly, sitting her down. 'Stop it! This won't help you.'

Her father tied her up. But as he looked up . . . was that a smile on his face?

'Ah, this takes me back,' said Umbra as Vi felt her mother struggle against their restraints. 'The problem today is that everyone is in such a rush, they forget the old ways.'

A giant timer appeared on the screen with a ten-minute countdown. Vi was sure she heard Robert grunt approvingly.

'I am going to slowly lower you into the tank below,' Umbra explained. 'Your whole body will be submerged, leaving only your heads above water. In that tank are fifteen hundred mutant piranhas. From where you are sitting, you will have the perfect view of them eating you. And should you still be alive in ten minutes, you'll have a ringside seat as I blow this whole place to smithereens.'

Umbra's satisfied laugh reverberated around the tower.

'So classy,' Robert sighed.

The transmitter on Robert's jacket suddenly bleeped.

'Uh, Sir Charge, front gate here – we have a problem,' the voice on the other end said. 'I don't . . . I don't really know how to explain it.'

'Try,' said Robert plainly.

'Well . . . OK,' the voice said. 'Someone who looks like a giant bat is attacking us with custard pies and a guy with two heads is trying to stop a clown from shooting everyone. And this woman in a catsuit has just done the worst fart . . .'

'I'll be right there,' Robert said with a sigh. 'How far away are you, boss?'

'A few minutes,' Umbra said. 'But first I'm going to sit back and watch our guests get devoured by my fish.'

'Excellent. Everything is going according to plan,' Robert said, handing the Neurotrol to Mick and looking straight at Vi. 'Just like I knew it would.'

Again, he locked eyes with his daughter before leaving the room. What was he trying to say?

'Well, now,' Umbra continued. 'I believe it's time to . . . and then . . . I'll . . . revenge . . . world . . . mine . . .'

With a fizzle and a crack, Umbra's face flickered away.

'Vi!' Russell's voice came over the walkie-talkie in her pocket. 'Vi – I've jammed the communication channel. Umbra can't see or hear you. Now's your chance to escape. I'm trying to override the platform now . . .'

Vi smiled. Nice one, Russell. With a jolt, the platform started a creaking descent towards the piranhas.

Vi looked at the clock. Nine minutes and fifty-six seconds. She reached around to the back of her jeans. She pulled the Eye-Spy carefully into her hand. She looked at Mick standing guard in the corner.

'Everyone stay very still,' she whispered. 'I'm going to cut these ropes, but you mustn't move. Keep talking, otherwise that guy will know something is up.'

'George,' said Easter softly. 'I'm so, so sorry.'

'Why didn't you just tell me?' George replied. 'Why the lies?'

'Because . . . because I thought you wouldn't love me if you knew who I really was.'

Easter started to sob softly. Vi felt George's fingers reach for her mother's.

'Susan . . . Easter . . . Agent Lynx,' he said, 'it

doesn't matter what you call yourself. I know exactly who you are. You are the woman I love. Nothing can change that.'

Vi could almost feel her mum's insides go mushy.

'I love you so much, George,' she sobbed.

'I love you too, whoever you are,' George sniffed back.

'When all this is over, I'm going to marry you, George Sprout,' she gushed.

'I haven't asked you yet,' said George shyly. 'So you'll just have to wait.'

'Oh George.'

'Oh Susan.'

'Oh George.'

'Oh Easter.'

'Oh . . .'

'Oh, gimme a break,' said Vi as she felt her way around the numbers on the watch. She set it to number five, the blade. She pressed the button and felt a small knife pop out of her watch. She held it to her ropes and sawed through them with a few strokes – within moments, she was free. Quick as a flash, she stood up and set the watch to one o'clock: tranquillize.

'Oh gosh – no, no, no – you don't understand,' whispered Mick, holding his hands up. 'I'm here to—'

'Mick – chill,' said Vi, firing a tranquillizing dart straight at the burly henchman. The dart landed in his tattooed arm and felled him like a jelly tree.

'Russell,' she said, grabbing her walkie-talkie, 'Russell – can you stop this platform?'

'Give me a minute,' said Russell. 'I've slowed it down, but I can't stop it. This system is so old – does no one update their software any more?'

'Russell!' Vi hissed.

'OK, OK,' said Russell.

Vi freed Mr Sprout and helped him to his feet.

'Great,' said Easter, lifting her hands behind her. 'Let's get out of here.'

Valentine looked at the clock. Eight minutes and forty-seven seconds. There was time.

'No,' said Vi simply.

'What?' said Easter. 'What do you mean, no?'

'I mean I'm not letting you go until we get something straight,' she said.

'Valentine . . .' George said, as the platform continued its slow descent. 'We don't have much time.'

'This won't take long,' said Vi. 'Mum. I want to go to Rimmington Hall. I want to be a spy. You have to let me.'

'No, I do not,' Easter huffed.

'Yes, you do,' said Vi. 'Because unless Russell stops this, you'll be eaten by mutant piranhas and I won't need your permission anyway.'

Easter let out a big huff.

'You were right,' Vi said, crouching down to her mum. 'This is dangerous. I don't know how to be a good spy. But Rimmington Hall can teach me. This week has been crazy – and I still want to do this more than ever. But I need you.'

'I don't want this life for you,' Easter insisted.

'But *I* do,' said Valentine. 'So teach me how to do it well. You're the best, Agent Lynx. Please let me learn from you.'

Easter looked at the approaching piranhas, then at her daughter.

'OK,' she sighed. 'OK.'

'Great,' said Vi brightly, cutting her mother free as the platform continued to descend. 'Now let's get out of here before we're all blown up.'

'I'm so proud of you, Valentine,' said Easter, hugging her daughter. 'Although if you ever get chocolate on my furniture again, it will be the last thing you do.'

Vi smiled and hugged her back. They were going to be all right.

So long as they escaped an exploding power station.

'We need to get the Neurotrol,' said Vi, running down the steps towards Mick's unconscious body. 'Before Umbra gets here.'

'Too late,' came a voice from the shadows, the now familiar sound of a trigger being cocked accompanying the greeting.

Vi looked over to the semi-darkness from the staircase. It was hard to make anything out in the gloom, but she could just pick out a hooded figure.

'Umbra,' said Easter. 'Clearly I need to eliminate you better this time.'

'Easter Day,' Umbra replied, reaching for Mick's unconscious body. A gloved hand pulled the Neurotrol from his pocket. 'I really think it's my turn.'

'Nooooo!' came a sudden shout from the steps. It was George running – or the closest thing any Sprout did to it – towards Umbra. His arms were flailing, his legs were wobbling. 'I won't let you . . . I . . .'

He was silenced by a single punch from Umbra, which dropped him to the floor.

'Looks like you're losing your killer touch, Easter. Perhaps we'd better give you some practice?' said Umbra gleefully. Vi saw the Neurotrol light up. 'Easter Day?'

'Yes,' said her mother, suddenly snapping to attention like a soldier.

'Eliminate Valentine Day. Then eliminate Easter Day.'

Vi looked over at her mother, who turned and looked murderously at her.

'Eliminate Valentine Day,' she repeated, striding towards Vi. 'Eliminate Easter Day.'

'Mum! No!' Vi cried, backing down the steps.

'Eliminate Valentine Day,' Easter repeated again.

'Mum! Mum – it's me!' Vi gabbled, trying to back down the steep staircase. She heard Umbra laughing softly in the shadows as Easter lunged forward and grabbed her, putting her hand over her mouth.

'Mum! Stop!' Vi shouted behind Easter's fingers, trying to get enough volume to control the Neurotrol herself. 'Mum, please listen to me! You don't want to do this.'

But her mum's grip was firm. And her eyes were cold and empty. They climbed up higher and higher until they were level with the platform again.

'Eliminate Valentine Day,' she chanted, picking up Vi, dragging her to the access point and jumping on to the descending platform. She walked to the edge and dangled Vi over it. Vi looked down at the frenzy of snapping piranhas below.

'Don't worry, child,' said Umbra. 'At least you'll be together. In a few agonizing minutes you'll both be dead. It's like all my Easters have come at once.'

'Mum! Mum, please!' said Vi as the piranhas circled. But she was way up high, her voice out of the Neurotrol's range. 'Please! Russell! Russell – you need to stop the platform!'

'I'm trying,' Russell cried. 'This system is ancient. It's like something from the 1990s . . .'

'Eliminate Valentine Day,' Easter repeated. 'Eliminate Easter Day.'

'Easter, STOP!' boomed a voice across the room as Robert charged in and kicked the

Neurotrol from Umbra's left hand and the gun from the right.

Easter came to as if she'd been slapped.

'What . . . what's . . . what . . . ?' she burbled.

'Easter – get Valentine off there!' Robert commanded from down below.

'Robert . . . what are you—' Umbra shouted.

'It's over, Umbra,' Robert shouted back, holding up his gun. 'I'm here to take you down.'

'Don't be absurd,' Umbra hissed. 'You work for me.'

'Not any more,' said Robert. 'I work for the government.'

'What?' said Vi and Easter simultaneously as the platform continued its descent towards the tank.

'You traitor!' Umbra roared. 'You'd turn your back on me?'

'Yes, I would,' said Robert. 'Robbing banks is one thing. But robbing free will? You've gone too far. I should never have abandoned my child to follow you – you're a maniac. I've cut a deal. My freedom for yours. I used the Neurotrol to root you out so I can turn you over to the authorities. I stopped you attacking Vi at Autumn Leaves. I brought Easter here to trap you. I made sure Vi could escape. I promised my little girl I would keep her safe. And Robert Ford never breaks his promises.'

'We'll just have to see about that,' said Umbra, lunging at Robert and knocking the gun into the tank for a feeding frenzy. 'Easter – eliminate Valentine Day! Eliminate Easter Day!'

'No, Easter! Stop!' cried Robert as he exchanged blows with Umbra on the ground.

Vi looked down at the piranhas and up at her mum. Easter was confused – and her grip was loosening.

'Easter! Eliminate the child!' Umbra yelled, landing a kick in Robert's chest.

'No! Save her!' Robert shouted, springing back off the floor.

Easter lifted Vi up and down over the platform as the different commands were barked at the Neurotrol. But even her strong arms were tiring.

'Vi?' Russell's voice came over the walkie-talkie. 'Vi – it's not good news, I can't override the bomb program. It needs to be manually defused. You guys have four minutes to get out of there.'

'Kinda busy right now!' Vi shouted back as Easter's arms started to tremble. 'Really need you to stop this platform!'

'Still trying,' said Russell. 'This system is so old.'

'Drop her!' Umbra yelled.

'Hold her!' Robert yelled back.

But as Easter's hands trembled, it didn't matter who commanded her. She was losing her grip.

'Mum!' Valentine pleaded. 'Mum! Hold on!'

It was no use. With shaking arms and a muddled mind, Easter let go. Vi dropped, but instinctively her hands reached for the edge of the platform, catching it with her fingers before she could fall. She gripped the metal, looking below at her legs dangling over the manic piranhas, then above to her zombified mother shaking on the platform. Vi's fingers were burning. She knew she couldn't hold on for long . . .

'Someone help me!' Vi screamed, just as Robert reached Umbra and pinned the dark figure to the ground. 'I'm going to fall!'

'What are you going to do, Robert?' Umbra hissed. 'Hold on to me, or save your daughter? You can't do both.'

'DAD!' Vi screamed, her fingers straining to grip the platform.

Robert's head snapped around.

'Vi!' cried Robert. 'Hold on!'

'I can't!' cried Vi, her sweaty fingers starting to slip.

'What's it going to be, Robert?' whispered Umbra. 'Me or Valentine?'

Robert sprang to his feet, releasing Umbra, who immediately leapt up, sprinted through the open door and punched the button to close it. Umbra was gone.

'It's always going to be Valentine,' Robert said, pelting towards the stairs, grabbing the Neurotrol and tossing it to his henchman.

'Mick!' he yelled to the groggy henchman. 'Switch it off!'

Mick immediately deactivated the Neurotrol, extinguishing the light.

On the edge of the platform Vi's fingertips were on fire and her arms were trembling at the strain of holding her body weight.

'Please! Hurry!' Vi screamed. 'I can't hold on!'

This was it. She was done for. Her aching fingers slipped off the smooth surface and she prepared herself to fall to her death . . .

But as her fingers surrendered their strength, Vi felt a firm grip on her wrist. She looked up.

Her mum was dangling upside down over the edge of the platform.

'It's OK, baby, I've got you,' she smiled. 'I've always got you.'

The platform jolted as it continued its clunky descent past the last access point on the stairs. Almost immediately they both started to fall.

'Argh!' Easter screamed. 'I haven't got her! I haven't got her! Robert! George! Henchman guy! Someone! Hurry!'

Vi heard her dad charge up the steps towards them. He threw himself off the stairs and on to the platform, grabbed Easter's ankles and with a heave, pulled them both back from the edge. Vi finally drew a breath. They were safe on the platform. But the piranhas were getting closer.

'Russell!' Vi shouted into the walkie-talkie. 'Russell – you have to stop this thing!'

'I can't!' said Russell, 'I don't know—'

'Control, Alt, Delete,' came a voice from the stairs.

'What was that?' Russell replied.

'Control, Alt, Delete,' George Sprout shouted more loudly, holding his groggy head. 'Press Control, Alt, Delete!'

'OK . . .' said Russell as the platform carried on towards the piranhas. They were only centimetres away now. Vi felt two pairs of strong arms around her as her parents held her. At least they would all be together for their last few moments. Vi shut her eyes as the bottom of the platform hit the water. She felt her parents' grasp tighten around her and . . .

The platform stopped.

'It worked!' Russell shouted. 'Dad – it worked!'

'Never fails,' mumbled Mr Sprout. 'Did you know it was invented by programmer David J. Bradley in 1981?'

'We've got you,' said Robert, hugging Vi close. 'You're safe.'

'Not exactly,' came Russell's anxious voice. 'The whole system is rebooting. I can't open your door. The bomb's going to explode any second! There's nothing I can . . . what . . . wait a minute . . . what are you doing here? Be careful with that, you'll . . .'

Suddenly, a blast ripped through the wall. Vi waited for the power station to collapse around them. But it didn't. And as the smoke cleared, a wonderfully welcome voice cut through it.

'Well, looks like we got here just in time,' said Nan, appearing through the hole.

'If in doubt, blow it up,' said a grinning Desmond, holding a detonator behind her. 'Come on – Felicity's working on the bomb. Let's get you out of here.'

With Russell back in control, the platform winched up to the last level. Vi and her parents jumped off and ran down the stairs. Vi looked up at the timer. They had twenty seconds to get out of the building.

'Let's go,' said Robert, as Mick picked up George and ran through the hole.

They raced down the corridor until they met Felicity, who was rubbing her hands together in satisfaction.

'ALL DONE,' she said. 'BOMB DEFUSED. IT WAS THE BLUE WIRE.'

'Er, darling,' said Desmond. 'I told you to cut the *red* wire . . .'

'EXACTLY,' smiled Felicity. 'I DID WHAT YOU SAID. I CUT THE BLUE WIRE.'

'Hurry!' yelled Vi, as they raced towards the open exit, Easter holding Vi's hand and Robert just behind. They still had a few seconds. They were going to make it. They were—

Smack!

A piece of crumbling brickwork fell on Vi's head and shoulder, severing her grip from her mother, who was running so fast she was several metres ahead before she could stop to see what had happened. The world went blurry as Vi sank to her knees . . .

'Valentine!' she heard Easter shout. 'Valentine – NO!'

Through her haze, Valentine felt something grab her close before she was knocked to the ground.

'I've got you!' Robert shouted as a thundering explosion went off all around them, covering Vi's body with his own as the power station was rocked to its core. For a moment, it seemed as though the whole world were collapsing on top of them. Valentine felt her dad absorb blow after blow as the bricks and pipes and whatever was left of Norton Power Station rained down on them and he shielded her from the debris.

And then . . . everything went quiet.

Vi opened her eyes. Everything hurt. That meant she was alive. But her father was horribly still. The corridor they'd been running through had been largely destroyed. It was only just about standing. Although judging by the creaking overhead, not for very long.

'Dad,' she said, wriggling her way from beneath his body. 'Dad?'

'Valentine!' Easter screamed, clambering over the brickwork to get to her. 'Are you OK?'

'I'm fine,' she said. 'But Dad . . . he . . .'

'He saved you. I saw.'

Easter dropped to her knees next to Robert's body. Was he . . .

'Robert? Robert?'

Easter turned him over and listened to his chest.

'He's alive,' she said. 'Just unconscious. We need to shock him back into . . .'

And without further explanation, she slapped him hard across his face.

'Owwwwwww,' Robert groaned. 'That takes me back . . . Hello Easter . . .'

'Get up,' Easter commanded, putting his arm around her shoulder and dragging him to his feet. 'We need to get you out of here. The whole building is about to collapse.'

'Still trying to tell me what to do,' Robert smirked.

'Still haven't learnt how to kill you,' Easter groaned as they made their way across the rubble towards the doors beyond.

'Hurry,' said Vi as the structure groaned around them. 'I think it's going to—'

With an almighty crack, the wall above them started to come down.

'Leave me,' said Robert groggily, sinking to his knees. 'Save yourselves . . .'

'You really are a complete idiot,' muttered Easter, putting her arms around Robert's upper body. 'Vi – grab his legs.'

Vi picked up her Dad's ankles behind her and she and Easter carried him through the collapsing building, moving as quickly as the uneven terrain allowed. Vi looked up as a terrifying groan went off above them. The whole power station was creaking.

'That way!' Easter commanded, gesturing to a field beyond the doors. 'Hurry!'

They charged out of the opening and burst into the fresh air, running across to the green grass with Robert between them. Just as they placed him on the grass, there was an almighty cracking sound behind them. Vi turned to watch. The tower started to buckle in on itself. And not half a heartbeat later, the entire Norton Power Station collapsed in a heap of dust.

'You're in big trouble,' said Easter, looking sternly at Vi.

'I know,' sighed Vi. 'You're furious with me . . .'

'It's not me you need to worry about,' said Easter. 'Just think what the town council are going to say when they realize they have to change their "Home to the Norton Power Station" sign.'

Vi looked at her mum. She was grinning. They both burst out laughing as Easter pulled Vi in for a massive hug.

'Thank you,' Easter whispered in her hair. 'Thank you for saving me.'

'Thank you for letting me,' said Vi, squeezing her mum. They were going to be OK.

'Easter!' a bruised George Sprout cried, leading the charge of Silver Service and EVIL. Siren was first to Robert's side.

'I'd give you mouth to mouth,' she smiled. 'But my breath smells like a portaloo.'

Robert grinned up at her as Easter and Mr Sprout hugged.

Russell rushed over with his laptop.

'Are you OK?' he asked Vi, handing her a tissue for her bleeding head.

'I am,' nodded Vi. 'Thanks for your help in there.'

'Any time,' Russell smiled.

'Everyone all right?' asked Indy.

'We're OK, thanks, Nan,' panted Vi. 'But how did you find us?'

'Two things,' said Indy. 'One, we investigated the coded chatter on the CobWeb about this place. We were deeply suspicious when a large order for mutant piranhas was delivered yesterday. And two, I put a tracking device in your Eye-Spy. What can I say? Once a spy, always a spy.'

'Nan!' grinned Vi. Although with the life she was hoping to lead, perhaps it was a good thing that people were watching out for her.

'Oh Susan, I thought I'd lost you,' George sobbed, holding Easter's head in his hands.

'Never,' said Easter. 'I love you, George Sprout.'

'I love you, Susan,' said George, stroking her face.

'George?' said Mum dreamily.

'Yes, Susan,' said George sappily.

'The name's Day,' she said. 'Easter Day.'

And she took George in her arms, bent him over backwards and gave him a long, passionate kiss.

'Woowaaweeewahh,' George said as Easter pulled away.

Vi smiled at Russell. That was gross. But good gross.

Vi looked up and saw three approaching figures pacing across the grass. It was the SPIDER agents.

'Vi,' whispered Robert urgently, pulling his daughter down to him. 'I have to tell you something. Do not trust anyone in SPIDER. We suspect – we're pretty sure, in fact – that one of these three – The Cardinal, Wolf or Honey B . . . is Umbra.'

'What?' gasped Vi instinctively. But then logic crept up behind it. The SPIDER agents were desperate to get their hands on the Neurotrol. What if they weren't trying to stop Umbra? What if one of them actually *was* Umbra?

'What happened here?' panted Honey B,

breathless as she reached them. 'I came as soon as I heard – are you all OK?'

Easter gave her best friend a hug.

'We're fine,' she said. 'Thanks to Vi.'

Honey turned and looked at her goddaughter.

'Well done, Vi,' she said, giving her a big hug. 'The world is very lucky to have you.'

'Thanks, Aunty Honey,' said Vi cautiously. 'How did you get here so fast?'

'Protocol dictates that we investigate any unusual activity,' said The Cardinal, coming up behind her. 'I was on my way to SPIDER HQ when I got the call, brought the chopper straight here.'

'I was in the area – I was coming to see you guys,' said Honey B.

'It doesn't matter how we got here, it matters that you let Umbra get away,' growled The Wolf. 'Did you get a look at his face? Or her face?'

Vi looked between the three SPIDER operatives. One of them was lying. And she was going to find out which.

'Yes,' said Robert at the same time that Vi said, 'No.'

'What happened to the Neurotrol?' The Cardinal barked. 'Do you have it?'

Vi and Robert looked at each other and then at Mick, who winked and patted his pocket.

'It's in there,' said Vi, pointing at the heap of rubble that used to be the power station. 'Good luck finding it.'

'You will come to SPIDER HQ and tell us everything you know,' said The Cardinal. 'You'd better get your stories straight.'

'The story is that my granddaughter completed her first mission!' Nan cried, hugging Vi. 'You did it! You stopped Umbra!'

Easter came over and Robert instinctively stepped back.

'Robert,' she said stiffly.

'Easter,' he replied just as stiffly.

'You saved Valentine,' she said. 'And for that . . .'

'Look, please,' said Robert modestly, holding up his hands. 'No big speeches of gratitude, it's what any father would do.'

Easter made a noise like a kettle boiling.

'Gratitude?' she screamed. 'For nearly getting us all killed? I was going to say that for saving Valentine, I won't kick your butt, but now I'm not so sure.'

'Oh, I'd like to see you try,' Robert puffed up.

'Mum!' Vi interrupted. 'Dad! Just . . . just chill.'

Her parents stopped, mouths still open. Then both took a breath. And then both of them backed down. It was a start.

'You did it,' said Russell, grinning in George's arms.

'*We* did it,' said Vi proudly, looking at her patchwork family. Yes, they were weird. But when they worked together, they were actually pretty awesome.

They made their way back to the car park. As Russell got into the car, Vi remembered the broken Agadoo sitting in their boot. She looked over to the minibus, where the Silver Service were enjoying a much-deserved flask of tea and slices of cake. She quickly ran over to them.

'Desmond?' Vi whispered. 'Could I ask you a favour?'

CHAPTER 19

The rest of the week went by in a bit of a blur. On Thursday, George moved back to the house from the shed, and Vi and Russell were given handfuls of cash to go to the movies and bowling and Laser Quest and anything else that would keep them out of the house. Easter and George said they needed lots of time to talk.

On Friday, Vi was picked up by helicopter to spend the morning at SPIDER's top-secret HQ being quizzed by the agents on what she knew about Umbra and the Neurotrol, which she insisted was very little. She wasn't about to tell SPIDER anything. That information would have to keep for another day.

On Friday afternoon, after a successful mission and with Easter's permission, Vi sat her entrance exams to Rimmington Hall at home via Zoom. They were super-tough – she wasn't at all sure she'd correctly calculated the number of bullets in 427 rounds of ammunition, nor successfully convinced a criminal overlord to make a donation to a charity collector. She was exhausted – so on Saturday Vi had planned to have a big sleep in. But an early doorbell called her out of bed. She hoped she knew who it was, so ran to answer it before anyone else got up. And she was right.

'Here you go, my dear,' said Desmond, delivering her package.

'You're sure it all works?' said Vi, smiling.

'Oh yes,' said Desmond with a twinkle in his eye. 'I even made a few slight . . . modifications. I hope they help. Just . . . be careful with the red button.'

'Thanks, Desmond,' said Vi, giving him a hug.

'Good luck!' said the kindly inventor. 'Let me know how you get on – see you on Monday?'

'Can't wait,' smiled Vi as Desmond got back on a mobility scooter and whizzed off rather faster than Vi had seen one travel before. She went up the stairs and knocked gently on Russell's door.

'Russell?' she said. 'Are you awake?'

'I am now,' said a sleepy voice inside.

Vi opened the door. But instead of walking in herself, she sent the delivery first.

'*Good morning, Russell Sprout*,' Agadoo chimed. '*Come on and do the conga.*'

'AGADOO!' Russell cried. 'What . . . how . . . why . . . ?'

'Here,' said Vi, handing over the remote control. 'He's good as new. Better, perhaps.'

'But how did you . . .' Russell asked, checking all Agadoo's controls and confirming that he was fully restored to working order.

'I can't take the credit,' she said. 'It was Desmond. You should hang out with him. I think you guys would get on really well.'

'What does this red button do?' he asked, peering at the new remote control.

'No idea,' said Vi. 'But if I know Desmond, I wouldn't test it here.'

'Thanks!' said Russell, his geeky little face lit up with joy. 'To . . . Desmond, I mean.'

'Of course,' said Vi. 'I'm sure . . . Desmond would be very happy to know you're pleased.'

'Wow!' puffed George, appearing in the door frame, his arm around Easter in her dressing gown. 'This is outstanding! But if we're going to make BlitzBotz, we're going to have to motor . . .'

'I'll just call Mum!' said Russell, running downstairs to the phone.

'Quickly!' shouted Mr Sprout, sprinting towards the shower and kissing Easter as he went. Vi had a hug with her grinning mum. It felt good to see everyone happy.

'Hi Mum! It's me!' said Russell brightly down the phone as Vi and Easter wandered into the kitchen. 'Me! Russell. We're going to be at BlitzBotz in about thirty minutes, so we'll meet you at the— Oh.'

Vi looked at her mum. Easter groaned and shook her head.

'OK,' said Russell, his shoulders dropping. 'But Lucas could come too, we've got enough tickets. He'd really enjoy it, it's got loads of robots and there are burgers and ice cream and – Oh . . . OK. No, I understand, Lucas's spelling homework is important too. Maybe you could just come for my battle and then . . . Yeah, I know the traffic is really bad on a Saturday, but . . . OK. No, I'm not being difficult. Say hey to Lucas from— Bye, then.'

Russell hung up the phone, which already had

a flat dial tone coming out of the other end. Vi felt sick for him. Her parents had their issues. But they'd never let her down like that.

'Hey Russ,' Easter said cheerily, gathering him into her arms. 'After BlitzBotz, let's all go out for Chinese food.'

'Don't worry about it,' mumbled Russell, shuffling his feet. 'Anyway, Vi's got her party.'

A car horn beeped outside. Vi walked to the front door and opened it up. There were Tom and Sally. In their limo. They'd come to take her to BlitzBotz.

'What party?' Easter snapped, following her. 'We never discussed you going to any—'

'Mum, chill,' said Vi, looking at Russell who was holding back tears. 'I've got this.'

Vi looked at the fancy car. This was it. Her ticket to be in with the most popular kids at school. All she had to do was get in the car.

She walked to the end of the driveway.

'Hey,' said Tom, pulling down his shades. 'Nice threads.'

'Yeah,' said Sally. 'PJs are soooo in . . . but go and get dressed. We need to party.'

'Thanks,' said Vi. 'But I'm not coming with you.'

'What?' said Tom, peering over his shades.

'I'm not coming with you,' Vi repeated. 'I'm not coming to your party. I'm going to BlitzBotz with . . . with my family.'

She turned around to see Easter and George, their arms around Russell in the doorway.

'But . . . family is so . . . out,' said Sally. 'You don't want to be out again, do you, Vi?'

Vi smiled at Tom and Sally and took a step back.

'Actually, yes,' she said. 'Turns out that I really, really do.'

'Rejection,' said Sally. 'That is soooo out.'

'Oh – and, Tom,' Vi called as she walked back to the house.

'Yeah,' said Tom, looking over his shades. Actually, his eyes weren't anything special at all.

'Agadoo is going to whip your robot's butt,' she said, smiling at Russell. Russell smiled back. That felt good.

And with that, she ran back into her home, accepted a hug from her smiling mum and charged upstairs to get ready for BlitzBotz.

'YES!!! GO ON, AGADOO!!!!' Vi screamed as Agadoo picked up another robot, spun it above his head and threw it out of the arena.

'Go on, boys!' Easter shouted. 'Rip off its head! Pull out its guts! Kick it where it hurts! Smash it with . . .'

Easter tailed off as she noticed nearby parents looking at her strangely.

'Er . . . well played,' she said, clapping politely and sitting back down as Agadoo rammed another opponent into a large pit in the far left corner of the battleground. The crowd cheered.

'And that's another victory for Agadoo!' the announcer declared as George and Russell gave each other a high five in the control room, beamed live on a huge screen. 'In a few minutes we will have the Grand Final, where our two undefeated robots, Agadoo and Ripsaw, will go head to head to see who will be crowned BlitzBotz champion!'

'Yes!' fist-pumped Vi.

A familiar face made its way towards where she and Easter were sitting.

'Hi Vi,' said Robert, kissing her head and distributing four giant foam fingers. 'Hello Easter.

Thank you for the invitation.'

'Hello Robert,' said Easter with something almost like a smile. 'Glad you could make it.'

Vi knew her parents weren't going to be best friends anytime soon. But at least they were making the effort to be civil. That was progress.

'How's the lad doing?' Robert asked, taking a sip of Vi's blue slushie before pulling a face.

'He's in the final,' said Vi proudly. And she was proud. Really proud.

'Good boy,' said Robert admiringly. 'Um, Easter . . . I have something for you.'

He handed Mum a brown envelope.

'What's this?' asked Easter cautiously.

'Divorce papers,' said Robert. 'I had them drawn up. I've signed everything. I hope you enjoy your second marriage better than your first.'

Easter opened the envelope and read the papers inside.

'Thank you, Robert,' she said with a genuine smile.

'You're welcome, Easter,' said Robert with a small nod of his head.

Vi grinned at her parents. Finally, they were being grown-ups.

The question was, for how long?

A saxophone started playing nearby. Vi smiled as she saw Siren wiggle her way across the rows. As she came closer, Vi noticed a shiny New Leaf Badge sparkling on her evening gown.

'Hi Easter,' said Siren, extending a gloved hand. 'We haven't been formally introduced. We met that night you foiled me stealing the Venus de Milo. I remember, because it was around the time I had that infected wart. Robert asked me along. I hope you don't mind.'

'Not at all,' said Easter, blinking furiously. Vi smiled at her mum's tell.

Loud music started blaring around the arena.

'And now!' the announcer cried as the lights dimmed, 'It's time for the ultimate showdown! In the red corner, driven by George and Russell Sprout, he's our matey from 1980, iiiiiiitttt's AGADOO!'

Agadoo came whizzing into the arena to some awful eighties song about pushing pineapples. But Vi didn't care – she and her whole family went nuts as Agadoo spun around the centre of the battleground.

'And in the blue corner!' the announcer

shouted. 'Controlled by Tom Parker, it's mean, it's nasty, it's . . .'

'Sally?' Vi suggested, making Easter spit her burger.

'That was soooo in,' her mum grinned.

'Oh Em Gee,' grinned Vi.

'It's RIPSAW!' the commentator bellowed to an appreciative roar from the crowd as Ripsaw rolled into the arena, a chainsaw buzzing in front of him.

'The battle will last two minutes,' the announcer shouted. 'You have one mission. To Blitz! That! Bot!'

The arena erupted into hysterical cheering as they counted down with the announcer. Vi felt a tickle of nerves in her stomach. She didn't want Agadoo to be blitzed. Not any more.

'3 . . . 2 . . . 1,' the crowd cried as the two robots blasted out of their corners towards one another.

'GO ON, AGADOO!' Vi screamed, as Ripsaw's chainsaw swept perilously past Agadoo's left wheel. She watched on the big screen as Russell expertly manoeuvred his bot around the arena, avoiding the fire blasts, open pits and other hazards placed around the floor.

But while Tom might have been a smarmy idiot, he too was an expert roboteer and no sooner had Agadoo escaped Ripsaw's clutches than he flipped over and headed back towards Russell's bot.

'It's early days, but it looks as though our reigning champ has the upper hand as Agadoo struggles to avoid the mighty Ripsaw,' the commentator opined.

'Oh, shut up,' said Vi under her breath, her heart pounding as Agadoo escaped another swipe of the chainsaw.

'Come on, Russell, come on,' she urged, willing Russell to teach Tom the lesson he so richly deserved.

'Oooooof,' the crowd groaned as the chainsaw passed Agadoo for a third time, this time causing sparks as it came into contact with the robot's metal frame.

'You can run, but you can't hide!' the commentator sang.

'Oh, shut up!' Easter and Vi shouted together.

Vi looked at the big screen. Russell wiped his sweaty brow. He headed for the button on the side wall that would open the pit beneath Ripsaw.

But suddenly, a flame shot out of it, forcing Russell to swerve Agadoo into a corner to avoid being set on fire.

'Oh no,' said Robert behind Vi. 'Not that way, fella. You'll be . . .'

'Trapped!' squealed the commentator as Ripsaw closed in on Agadoo, who was now caught between the pit and the flames, with Ripsaw blocking the only clear path out. 'It looks like Agadoo . . . is Aga-done for!'

'OH, SHUT UP!' the whole family shouted together.

'The button,' said Vi under her breath, willing Russell to hear her. 'Hit the red button.'

She watched Russell and George have an urgent conversation in the control box. She looked to the other screen where Tom was staring gleefully as his robot rolled towards Agadoo with the chainsaw. She looked back at the Sprouts. George shrugged and put his hands up. Russell's thumb hovered over the red button.

Ripsaw was now only centimetres away from Agadoo, his whirring blade getting closer to Agadoo's certain destruction.

'Hit the button!' Vi hissed. On the other

screen, Tom grinned like a panther going in for the kill. What was Russell waiting for?

Just as the crowd was baying for Agadoo's battery acid, Vi saw the Sprouts simultaneously push their glasses up their noses, hold hands and punch the red button together. Immediately, Agadoo's arms retracted inside his body.

'What use is that?' Easter cried. 'He can't defend himself without his arms.'

No sooner had the words left her lips than two rocket launchers emerged from Agadoo's arm sockets.

'But he can defend himself with those,' cried Vi. 'FIRE!'

Russell and George grinned at each other, clasped hands and hit the red button again, firing a point-blank hit on Ripsaw.

KER-POW!!!

A deafening explosion filled the arena.

'What the—' the commentator shouted. 'What just happened? Are there any survivors?'

The crowd went quiet as smoke seeped up from the arena floor, obscuring the view.

'I don't think he should have hit the button,' whispered Easter.

Vi sat transfixed. What had Desmond done?

But as the smoke cleared, an unmistakable sound rang out.

'AGA-DOO-DOO-DOO,' belted the little robot, spinning on the spot next to the pile of smouldering parts that used to be Ripsaw.

'YYYYYYYEEEEEEEESSSSSSSS!' screamed Vi, jumping to hug her mum, her dad and her . . . Siren . . . as Russell and George went nuts in the control room. 'If in doubt, blow it up! Nice one, Desmond.'

'Well, that's what you call an explosive finale,' chuckled the commentator, as Tom stormed off the other screen. 'And what do you call the undisputed BlitzBotz champion? Well we call him . . . AGADOO!'

'GO, RUSSELL!' Vi shouted, punching the air with her giant foam finger as they all stood up to go and congratulate the Sprouts on their epic victory.

'We'll leave you to it,' said Robert, standing up and putting his arm around Siren. 'We have lunch plans.'

'Thai food,' smiled Siren. 'My favourite. I can pick pad thai out of my teeth for days. My upper jaw gets like a worm farm.'

Vi smiled and gave them both a hug.

'See you next week?' Vi called as she raced towards Russell and George.

'You'd better believe it,' Robert called back.

'Russell! You did it!' cried Easter, picking Russell up and swinging him about.

'Careful,' grinned Russell. 'I'm not Mr Tilsley.'

'What?' asked Mr Sprout.

'Long story,' said Vi, giving him a big hug. 'Nice one. George.'

'Thanks, Vi,' grinned George, as Easter wrapped her arms around him and gave him a huge kiss.

Vi held up her hand to give Russell a high five. 'You won!'

'I did,' said Russell. 'And it was really cool having my family here to watch me. Well . . . I mean . . . your family . . . or . . .'

'Our family,' said Vi with a happy smile.

'Our family,' Russell agreed with a happy smile back.

'Ms Day. Mr Sprout. Valentine,' said an unfamiliar voice.

Vi turned around. Standing behind her was a middle-aged Indian lady wearing a dark blue trouser suit. Her short black hair sat in a neat bob around her face and her smiling brown eyes were framed with square, black glasses.

'Ms Direction!' said Easter. 'Everyone – Ms D is the head teacher at Rimmington Hall.'

Vi felt her stomach knot. Was this good news or bad?

'Good to see you,' Easter continued. 'Didn't have you down as a BlitzBotz fan.'

'I'm not,' said Ms Direction. 'I knew I'd find you here.'

'You know about BlitzBotz?' Vi asked.

'No,' said Ms Direction plainly. 'I've been following your every move since your grandmother registered you at birth. We place all applicants on our satellite tracking system.'

Vi shook her head. Spies. What were they like?

'Congratulations, Valentine,' Ms Direction smiled. 'You passed your assessment. We would be delighted to welcome you to Rimmington Hall in September.'

Vi shot a nervous look at Easter, whose jaw was clenched in something like a smile. George gave her a reassuring squeeze.

'Congratulations, darling,' said Easter, coming

to put her arm around Vi. 'You'll make a fantastic spy.'

'I've learnt from the best,' whispered Vi in her mum's ear. 'Thanks, Mum.'

'But I'm also here to talk to you, Mr Sprout,' said Ms Direction. 'You've come to our attention too.'

'Me?' said George, looking terrified.

'No,' smiled Ms Direction. 'Russell Sprout.'

'Thank goodness for that,' sighed Mr Sprout. 'The toughest mission I can face is getting my Year Sixes to finish their grammar homework.'

'Russell, we are seriously impressed with you,' said Ms Direction. 'We've seen your test results from the Tech Academy scholarship. Extraordinary. The signal jammer you constructed at the disco was inspired. And your programming at the power station was way beyond your years. You have many talents that we could utilize in our business.'

'Really?' Russell asked incredulously.

'Really,' confirmed Ms Direction. 'We were wondering if you might be interested in a place at Rimmington Hall?'

'Me?' said Russell, unable to believe his ears. 'At . . . spy school?'

'Yes. You,' smiled Ms Direction. 'What do you say?'

Russell looked up at his dad, who gave him a confirmatory wink.

'Is it . . .' Russell began. 'It is OK with you, Vi?'

Vi looked at her geeky, embarrassing nearly-stepbrother. Another seven years at school with him?

'Absolutely,' she grinned.

'Fantastic,' said Ms Direction. 'Then I'll see you both in September.'

Vi and Russell exchanged a happy smile. More exciting adventures were clearly on the way.

'Oh, Ms Direction,' she began. But Ms Direction had already disappeared.

'Right, you lot,' said Easter, clapping her hands. 'Let's go for Chinese food! We're celebrating!'

Vi resolved to enjoy this moment while it lasted. The second her mum got on the bathroom scales after a burger *and* an aromatic crispy duck tomorrow, there would be hell to pay . . .

'Yes,' said George nervously. 'Yes, we really should celebrate.'

'Well, then, let's go,' said Easter, but George held her back.

'Just a minute,' he said, nodding to Russell, who started to control Agadoo with the remote. The slightly battered robot rumbled forward and opened his claw hand. On the end of one of his fingers was Mum's engagement ring.

'Easter Day,' said George, dropping to one knee. 'Will you marry me? Again?'

Vi watched Easter's eyes fill with tears.

'Yes!' she cried, pulling George to his feet, spinning him around and nearly crushing him in her hug. 'Of course I'll marry you, George Sprout!'

Another gross kiss followed. But this time, Vi didn't mind. There were worse things than happy parents.

'Come on,' said Vi, as George put his arm around her and Easter put hers around Russell. 'I'm starving!'

The family skipped out of the arena, their dancing steps projected on to the big screen.

But not everyone was celebrating with them.

'Enjoy your victory for now,' said Umbra, watching the feed with a determined grimace.

'Because next time – and there will be a next time – I will get my Neurotrol. Make the most of Rimmington Hall while you can, Valentine Day. Because I promise you, I'm going to teach you a lesson you'll never forget . . .'

END OF MISSION 1